# World Yoshukai Karate Kobudo Organization Handbook

Grandmaster:
Soke Katsuoh Yamamoto

Directors:
Master Hiroaki Toyama
Master Mike Culbreth

# World Yoshukai Karate Kobudo Organization Handbook

Grandmaster:
Soke Katsuoh Yamamoto

Directors:
Master Hiroaki Toyama
Master Mike Culbreth

Edited By: Erik Hofmeister

Contributors:

| | |
|---|---|
| Ken Blumreich | Sherrie Hines |
| Russell Goetze | Josh McCullars |
| Robert Bishop | Buz Dale |
| Leo Gude | David Register |
| Benjamin Dawkins | Ajay Sharma |

1st Edition

Copyright © 2013 World Yoshukai Karate Kobudo Organization

ISBN-13: 978-0615848808 (World Yoshukai Karate Kobudo Organization)
ISBN-10: 061584880X

# Foreword

Yoshukai Karate can trace its lineage back to the founding fathers of karate in Okinawa over three hundred years ago. We are proud that World Yoshukai Karate Kobudo Organization is the only karate association recognized and certified by Yoshukai founder Grandmaster Katsuo Yamamoto. World Yoshukai Karate is recognized for extensive physical training, self-defense, self-control and respect for oneself and others. World Yoshukai students are noted for their perseverance, loyalty, dedication, respectful manners and strong hearts. Grand Master Yamamoto has founded an organization determined to provide quality instruction to anyone at any age.

The organization is led by Director Shihan Hiroaki Toyama and Director Shihan Mike Culbreth. We are very proud to have quality instructors and black belts in World Yoshukai, many of which are national champions and nationally ranked. They are both strong and supportive.

Hard traditional martial arts training with lots of emphasis on respect, manners, honesty and discipline are the backbone of a true Martial Artist. Yoshukai helps students to become well rounded individuals and well as karate students. Our teaching does not emphasize just one area but encompasses all areas such as kata, weapons, self-defense, breaking, point fighting and Japanese knock-down fighting (full contact).

Kaicho Hiroaki Toyama and Kaicho Mike Culbreth

# Introduction

This is the official training manual of the World Yoshukai Karate Kobudo Organization (WYKKO), as directed by Master Hiroaki Toyama and Master Mike Culbreth and overseen by Grandmaster Katsuoh Yamamoto. This manual is intended to be a definitive resource for the Yoshukai student and instructor and, along with the training video, should form the basis for unification of WYKKO techniques and principles. It is expected that the serious student will own a copy of this manual for reference and to guide their training throughout their time with WYKKO. This handbook is not intended to supplant training at an official WYKKO dojo.

# Table of Contents

# History and Background

## History of Karate

Martial arts have been in existence for as long as man has hunted and fought. The origins of the Asian martial arts are not well documented, but it is generally accepted that martial arts from India travelled into China. Legend holds that Bodhidharma, a Buddhist monk credited with bringing Zen to China, also brought and taught Shaolin kungfu in the 5th century CE. Regardless, there was significant cultural interaction between India and China, and martial arts were among the aspects of the cultures which were shared.

It is likely that, from China, organized styles of martial arts traveled to Japan and Okinawa. Okinawa is an island which lies to the south of Japan, halfway to Formosa (present-day Taiwan). It was its own kingdom, distinct from Japan and China, until the 16th century CE. At this time, the leaders of the Satsuma prefecture of Japan invaded Okinawa. The Okinawans did not fight, on the order of their king. Thereafter the Satsuma clan introduced a policy banning weapons to be owned by commoners. In each of the main cities of Okinawa, a unique unarmed fighting style began to be practiced by the commoners, typically within family lines. These were known as Shuri-te (from the Shuri district), Naha-te (from Naha city), and Tomari-te (from Tomari village), which together are known as Tode or Tote.

Shuri was the capital of Okinawa, and Shuri-te was practiced by many notables, particularly Gichin Funakoshi. Gichin Funakoshi was the founder of Shotokan karate and is generally credited with establishing the modern system of karate seen today. Gichin Funakoshi was born in Shuri, Okinawa in the year of the Meiji Restoration around 1868. He became close friends with the son of Ankō Asato, a karate and kendo master. Being trained in both classical Chinese and Japanese philosophies and teachings, Funakoshi became an assistant teacher in Okinawa. During this time, his relations with the Asato family grew and he began nightly travels to the Asato family residence to receive karate instruction from Ankō Asato.

Funakoshi had trained in both of the popular styles of Okinawan karate of the time: Shorei-ryu and Shorin-ryu. His style was influenced by kendo distancing and timing. Shotokan is named after Funakoshi's pen name, Shoto, which means "pine waves" or "wind in the pines". Kan means training hall, or house, thus Shotokan referred to the "house of Shoto". This name was coined by Funakoshi's students when they posted a sign above the entrance of the hall at which Funakoshi taught reading "Shoto kan". By the late 1910s, Funakoshi had many students, of which a few were deemed capable of passing on their master's teachings. Continuing his effort to garner wide-spread interest in Okinawan karate, Funakoshi ventured to mainland Japan in 1922. In 1936, Funakoshi built the first Shotokan dojo in Tokyo. In 1937, he changed the name of karate to mean "empty hand" instead of "China hand"; the two words sound the same in Japanese, but are written differently.

Anko Itosu was also a prominent figure in the early development of karate, predated Gichin Funakoshi by a generation. Itosu was trained in Naha-te, including the kata Kusanku and Chiang Nan. He broke those forms into smaller pieces, naming them the pinan forms, to make them easier for students to learn. Prior to Itosu, karate was taught in secret, usually passed down only within families or to closely trusted friends.

Itosu made his training available to the public, and therefore allowed karate to flourish as a popular form of training.

A discussion of formalized modern karate would not be complete without mention of judo and its founder, Jigaro Kano. Judo was the first 'modern' martial art, synthesized by Professor Kano from jujitsu. Professor Kano desired to create a system which trained not only the body, but the mind and the spirit, as well. Professor Kano introduced the modern kyu/dan grade system, where white belts were referred to as kyu and blackbelts referred to as dan. This system became expanded over the years to its current method of using color belts to represent the kyu grades. Gichin Funakoshi adopted the belt system of judo and applied it to his karate system.

## History of Yoshukai Karate

Dr. Tsuyoshi Chitose was born in 1898 near Naha City in Okinawa. His family had a long history of training in the martial arts, and growing up he studied the traditional Okinawan art of Tode. Chitose, through family connections, had access to the finest teachers Okinawa had to offer. He began his study at the age of seven under Aragaki Seisho, a teacher of Tode and extremely skilled in the use of bo and kama. Young Chitose spent over seven years with Aragaki Sensei until a disagreement caused him to leave Aragaki for other instruction around 1913. Chitose had spent most of his time on the kata Seisan, though he also was taught Sanchin and Niseishi.

His next teacher was Higashionna Kanryo, though it would only be for a short period as Higashionna passed away in 1915. In Shuri he studied under Motobu Chotoku, gaining knowledge in Unsu and Wansu. In Kadena (Nakigami District), he learned Chinto and Kusanku, and, along with Aragaki Ankichi, the katas Bassai and Ananko under Kyan Chotoku. At the Sogen Ji he learned the katas Jion, Jitte, Shihohai and Ryusan under Hanashiro Chomo.

Chitose spent two years in Tokyo enlisted as a member of the Imperial Guard Division (1918-1920), but when he contracted typhoid fever he had to return home to recover. Chitose took up teaching for a short while at the Okinawan Teachers College and by 1922 he was ready to head back to Japan to study medicine. He was accepted as a student at the Tokyo University Medical Center and became a doctor in 1924, then spent five years working in a hospital after graduation from medical school before he was accepted as a full doctor by the Japanese Medical Association. His field of study was obstetrics/gynecology. On his return to Tokyo he found Funakoshi Gichin had begun his teaching in Japan at the request of Judo's Jigaro Kano. Chitose would assist at times during these early days of karate as Funakoshi was getting established.

By 1945, he had 40 years of training and study and was now embarking on a new course in his karate. He opened his first dojo in 1946 and began teaching a new generation of students which would culminate in the creation of Chito Ryu. When Chitose opened his dojo, two eras of karate were crossing– the old Te of Okinawa and the new systemized ways of post war Japan. Chito Ryu means "method that goes back to the T'ang era in China about 1000 years ago," which Chitose designed to carry on the old Te of Okinawa. By 1950, Chitose was ready to retire from his medical practice and devote all his energy to promoting his art in a new era.

Mamoru Yamamoto was born on July 10th, 1938 in Shonai town on Okinawa. He had always wanted to be considered "strong." As a young man, he pursued athletics and excelled in track and field. When he was fifteen years old, he was attacked by a group of older boys, and although he tried to defend himself using the judo taught at his junior high school, he was defeated and beaten by the gang of ruffians. It was at this time he decided to start training in the art of karate. He began his karate by training in Chito-ryu under its originator, Tsuyoshi Chitose. In 1959, he opened his own school in Kitakyushu, Japan. In 1960, he began to train in kobudo to expand his martial arts understanding. From 1960 to 1963, Yamamoto was considered the top competitor in Japan. In 1963 Chitose pronounced him the Grandmaster of the Yoshukai style of karate. Initially, Yamamoto's style was called Chito-Ryu Yoshukan. Once he established his own association, the name was changed to Yoshukai, dropping the Chito-Ryu qualification.

## History of World Yoshukai Karate Kobudo Organization

Master Yamamoto sent Mike Foster, one of his most advanced students, to spread Yoshukai into the United States, in 1967. In 1969, Master Yamamoto sent Yuki Koda to the United States to work with Mike Foster. Yuki Koda opened a school in Birmingham, Alabama in 1975. Kiroaki Toyama started training in 1970 in Japan and promoted to Nidan before moving to the United States to continue expanding Yoshukai. It was around this time that Mike Culbreth began training in Yoshukai. In 1975, Mike Foster founded Yoshukai International Karate Association, breaking from Master Yamamoto. Yuki Koda continued under Master Yamamoto's direction to form the United State Yoshukai Karate Association. Yuki Koda continued to direct USYKA until his death in 1997. According to his wishes, his son David Koda became director of USYKA. Master Yamamoto wanted the highest-ranked Yoshukai instructor, Hiroaki Toyama, to direct the organization. Consequently, Master Yamamoto directed Hiroaki Toyama and Mike Culbreth to found the World Yoshukai Karate Kobudo Organization in 2000.

# Philosophy and Conduct

Yoshu can be translated to mean "raise up excellent people." Yoshukai can be translated to mean "association of continued improvement," although it is more commonly translated as "strive for excellence." The Yoshukai motto is rikki hitatsu, which translates to "make efforts and you will achieve." From both of these principles, it can be seen that continued effort, enthusiasm, practice, and diligence are key characteristics of any Yoshukai student. Yoshukai encourages personal excellence above and beyond competition or forcing students to perform to the standards of others. Individual improvement and progress is critical to advancement in Yoshukai. The pursuit of Yoshukai is lifelong, and a practitioner is always a student– learning, training, and focusing their skills.

The Yoshukai byword is nin, which translates to "patience." This is also a core concept to one's training. Students who wish to rush their training or hurry through the ranks are not exemplifying the concept of Yoshukai. The process of learning and training is more important than the goal of rank advancement, and this is exemplified in the concept of patience.

Yoshukai students should be humble with respect to their abilities, respectful of others (including peers, lower ranking students, and higher ranking students), courteous, show good sportsmanship during competitions, have solid integrity and strength of character, and exercise excellent self-control.

## Rules of the Dojo

As a traditional martial art, Yoshukai includes elements of not only physical training but mental and spiritual, as well. Certain rules are respected during training to help focus the student's mental energy to allow for the physical demands of training.

The student should bow when entering or leaving the training area. This shows respect to the dojo and the other students who train there. The student should bow when changing a line formation or moving from the line. Students should bow to the entrance of the training area when a senior rank enters or leaves for a training session. In most schools, this occurs whenever a black belt enters or leaves. For WYKKO events, this occurs whenever a Shihan rank black belt enters or leaves. This is to show respect to the high ranked student for their time during the training session. When greeting each other, Yoshukai students bow to each other and then shake hands with both hands. This is to show respect and also demonstrate that you have nothing to conceal in your other hand.

Students must show respect to their instructor and fellow students at all times. Therefore, students should always ask questions in a deferential, respectful manner. Students should not cross their arms over their chest or put their hands on their hips, as this implies a lack of readiness on the student's part to receive instruction (Masters may place their arms in whatever fashion they desire). Students should clasp their hands behind their back if they are at rest (yasume). There is no profanity or gum chewing allowed in the dojo.

Jewelry is not allowed during training. An exception may be made for a wedding band on an individual basis, with the Sensei's approval. This is for two reasons. First, any jewelry poses a potential risk of injury to the student or training partners. Second, jewelry denotes social status which is not relevant to the practice of Yoshukai.

If a student is late to class, they should sit in seiza and perform zarei and wait until the instructor calls on them to join class.

Other students, particularly those of higher rank, should be addressed as "Mr." or "Ms." followed by their last name. Instructors may be called "Sensei" followed by their last name. High ranking blackbelts may be referred to as "Shihan"– which means "quality instructor"– followed by their last name. Very high-ranking blackbelts may be addressed as "Master."

When seated, such as a judging table for a test, the highest-ranked student sits in the middle, flanked by the next highest-ranked, and so on.

A formal bow is undertaken when beginning and ending class. When performing a formal bow-in procedure, the highest-ranked student should lead the bow. All students face the front of the dojo (shomen) and the instructor give the command "seiza". Everyone kneels down with the left knee first, followed by the right knee. The instructor then says "Soke-ni rei" and everyone performs zarei. This is a bow to Soke Yamamoto. If Kaicho are not present, the instructor then says "Kaicho-ni rei" and everyone performs zarei. This is a bow to Master Toyama and Master Culbreth. If the Kaicho are present, they each have a bow directed to them by name. From there, each level of blackbelt has its own bow except for first and second degree blackbelts, who have a combined bow. Seventh degree and sixth degree blackbelts each have "Shihan-ni rei" as a command to bow. All remaining Shihan then have a "Shihan-ni rei" bow. Then a bow is given to fourth degree "Shihan-dai-ni rei" and third degree "Sempai-ni rei" students. Finally, first and second degree students receive "Yudansha-ni rei." If the individual leading the bows is the head instructor for the school, they receive a separate bow with the command of "Sensei-ni rei." If the individual leading the bows is a first or second degree blackbelt and is not the had instructor, and there are other first and second degree blackbelts, the individual leading bows receives "Yudansha-ni rei" and then all other first and second degree blackbelts receive a separate "Yudansha-ni rei" bow. In all cases, the highest ranked student of the level below that receiving the bow give the command to bow. For example, the highest-ranked third degree blackbelt calls "Shihan-dai-ni rei."

## How to Bow

There are two types of bow performed in Yoshukai– a standing bow or tachirei, and a kneeling bow or zarei. A bow is used to show respect and thanks, but does not indicate worship, submission, or idolatry. As Yoshukai students, we are learning not only a martial art but a way of life, and the etiquette and culture of Japan is integral to that understanding.

To execute tachirei, the student stands at attention with the feet pointed at 45 degree angles from touching heels. Keep the back and neck straight and bend from the waist. The fingers of each hand are together and go down along the creases of the pants. The student's eyes track down with the incline, neither looking down nor up. This should allow the student to keep a partner or opponent in sight. The depth and length of the bow depends on the circumstance, with a bow to a high ranked student held longer.

To execute zarei, the student must first kneel in seiza position. To do this, the student first kneels with the left knee, followed by the right knee, and rests back on their heels. In seiza, the big toe of one foot should cross over the big toe of the other foot. The hands are placed comfortably on the tops of the thighs. To execute the bow, slide the right hand down to the floor, keeping the fingers together and projecting the thumb out. Then slide the left hand down and touch fingertips and thumb tips together to form a triangle. Place the elbows on the floor and bend the upper body without bending the neck. The tip of the nose should be in the triangle formed by your hands, and you should stay seated on your heels as much as possible. After a 3-4 second count, lift the body and return first the left hand and then the right hand to your thighs. All students should come upright at the same time. This hand motion is undertaken so the hand which might grab a sword (the left) from your side is away from the sword for as short a time as possible. If a student is sitting in seiza and the instructor calls "yasume", the student executes one zarei and then can sit in a comfortable (i.e. cross-legged) position.

## The Five Precepts

The Five Precepts are rules to live by, not only in the dojo, but throughout your life. Yoshukai is not just a system of movements but also reflects mental and spiritual training and focus. Master Yamamoto devised the precepts which should serve the student throughout their training.

First precept: **Respect and Manners** (Reigi o omanzubeshi). As noted above, students must be respectful at all times and comport themselves well. Students should have respect for themselves, their fellow students, their instructors, and all of humankind in general. Courtesy flows from respect. Showing respect and manners and courtesy to others makes it less likely that a student will provoke a physical confrontation. Students should respond to questions directed at them with "Osu", "Sir" or "Ma'am."

Second precept: **Be Prudent in Action** (Taido o imashimubeshi). The student should never abuse the knowledge they learn studying Yoshukai. The skills acquired should only be used to defend oneself or others from harm, and never used to oppress or endanger others. Students should react appropriately when provoked. Someone grabbing the student is far different from someone brandishing a knife, and the response by the student should be scaled appropriately.

Third precept: **Be Prudent in Speech** (Gengo o tsutsushimubeshi). The student should always address others in a courteous fashion, and not use their speech to provoke confrontations. They must not use profanity, vulgarity, or curse in the dojo.

Fourth precept: **Keep High Spirited** (Iki o sakan ni subeshi). Throughout a student's training and life, it can be easy to become downhearted and feel overwhelmed. Keeping high spirited will help see a student through these difficult times. No matter how tired a student is, they should be enthusiastic and excited to be training in Yoshukai karate. Students should run if they have to move more than three steps. Students should kiai loud and with enthusiasm to show spirit. In training, students should attend class regularly to show their spirit and dedication to Yoshukai.

Fifth precept: **Keep Yourself Clean** (Seiketsu o mune to subeshi). The student should keep themselves both mentally and physically clean. The uniform should be clean and have the appropriate WYKKO patch and not be torn or damaged. The WYKKO Patch is worn on the right shoulder, just below the seam joining the sleeve to the body of the dogi. An unclean body is offensive to others both during training and outside of the dojo. A clean, clear mind is required to be receptive to the teachings of Yoshukai and to advance within the art.

# Training

Training in Yoshukai should be a regular, recurring practice for the student. Training can include a number of elements, including basic techniques, kata, sparring, conditioning, and self-defense. Each individual dojo may approach training in a slightly different fashion, and individual techniques will be taught during class periods.

## Kiai (気合)

Kiai can be translated as "concentrated or unified energy," and refers to a gathering of energy released in a single explosive focus of will. In martial arts, kiai is most commonly referred to as a short exhalation before or during a technique. This exhalation is often voiced as a powerful yell, but loudness is only one of many potential characteristics of a good kiai. Others include aligned body structure, focused will or intent, and proper breathing.

Kiai has several purposes in martial arts practice:

- To prime oneself for action.
- To startle or demoralize shy opponents.
- To protect the upper body from a strike. In this case, the kiai provides an escape route for air compressed by a strike as well as strengthening the intercostal muscles protecting the ribs and lungs.
- To protect the lower body from a strike by using the abdominal muscles and core strength to absorb the strike and protect internal organs.
- To concentrate the body's strength towards the execution of a powerful or difficult technique.
- To inspire spirit in oneself or fellow practitioners.

To execute a good kiai, proper attention must be paid to the breath (or *kokyu*). As an exercise, place both palms 2 to 3 inches above the navel. Then exhale several times in quick succession as if blowing out a candle. Notice the small contraction of the abdominal muscles supporting this exhalation--this is where a powerful exhalation, and in turn, a powerful kiai will originate. Once this feeling is comfortable, begin focusing on a relaxed inhalation that expands both the ribcage and the abdominal muscles. This focus will, over time, increase the volume of air contained in a single breath. Now, start coordinating this sharp exhalation with striking techniques. This is known as a "silent kiai," and it can quite effectively boost the technique's power, intensity, and focus.

To develop a strong voiced kiai, some experimentation is necessary to find a practitioner's optimal sound. Depending on the body's structure, the yell might be higher or lower in pitch. Generally speaking, practitioners often focus the explosion of sound from the throat, which can work, but it will often result in a hoarse or strained voice. A good kiai does not have to hurt the throat. Instead, concentrate the explosive character of the sound from the abdominal muscles. At first, the resulting sound may be a bit more hollow, but with experimentation in the pitch and breath intensity, almost any practitioner without vocal stress injuries will be able to produce a loud, piercing and resonant kiai.

## Kime (決め)

Kime is translated as "focus," and refers to the completion of a technique and the orientation of power on that technique. Kime can be composed of six elements:

- Mental Alertness: The student's mind concentrates on the tasks at hand.
- Execution of Technique: The ability to execute the proper body mechanics of karate. After the technique is thrown it must be retracted with the same attention to detail.
- Accuracy: This is the ability to execute a technique to the intended target in a repeatable fashion.
- Penetration: The ability to penetrate through a target surface, not just hitting the surface of the target.
- Muscle Manipulation: The body is first relaxed, then tense at exactly the point of impact, then relaxed again.
- Timing: All of the elements have to be combined in conjunction with the target, such as a moving opponent.

# Ni Ju Shichi No Kata

# 27 Movements

Start from the **ready stance** (Uchihachiji dachi).

1) **Upper block** with left hand (Hidari te jodan uke).

2) **Upper block** with right hand (Migi te jodan uke).

3) **Outside center block** with left hand (Hidari te chuudan soto uke).

4) **Outside center block** with right hand (Migi te chuudan soto uke).

5) **Inside center block** with left hand (Hidari te chuudan uchi uke).

6) **Inside center block** with right hand (Migi te chuudan uchi uke).

7) **Down block** with left hand (Hidari te gedan uke).

8) **Down block** with right hand (Migi te gedan uke).

9) **Center punch** with left hand (Hidari te chuudan zuki). **Kiai**.

10) **Center punch** with right hand (Migi te chuudan zuki). **Kiai**.

11) Right hand to tsuki position, **left hand punching to the right side** (Hidari te chuudan zuki). Look 45° to the right.

12) Left hand to tsuki position, **right hand punching to the left side** (Migi te chuudan zuki). Look 45° to the left.

13) **Left punch over right shoulder** and a simultaneous **right elbow strike** (Migi te embi). Look over your right shoulder.

14) **Right punch over left shoulder** and a simultaneous **left elbow strike** (Hidari te embi). Look over your left shoulder.

15) **Left elbow strike** to the chin (Hidari te embi).

16) **Right elbow strike** to the chin (Migi te embi).

17) Chamber for **left knife hand strike**.

**Left outward knife hand strike** to temple (Hidari te jodan soto shuto).

18) Chamber for **right knife hand strike**.

**Right outward knife hand strike** to temple (Migi te jodan soto shuto).

19) **Left upper palm heel strike** (Hidari te jodan shotei). **Kiai**.

20) **Right upper palm heel strike** (Migi te jodan shotei). **Kiai**.

21) Leaving right hand out, pull left arm horizontal in front of body and then execute an **elbow strike** to the left (Hidari te embi), drawing right hand back to tsuki. Look to the left.

22) Look straight ahead; reach out towards the front with right hand.

On the same count, twist into a **right leg shoulder stance** (Migi ashi zenkutsudachi at an angle) and execute a **left elbow strike** into your right hand (Hidari te embi).

23) Shifting back to a **ready stance** (Uchihachiji dachi) stack left arm on top of right arm and execute an **elbow strike** to the right (Migi te embi), drawing left hand back to tsuki. Look to the right.

Ni Ju Shichi No Kata

**Side view**

24) Look straight ahead, reach out towards the front with your left hand, twist into a **left leg shoulder stance** (Hidari ashi zenkutsudachi at an angle) and execute a **right elbow strike** into your left hand (Migi te embi).

25) Staying in a **left leg shoulder stance** (Hidari ashi zenkutsudachi at an angle), make a fist with your left hand and cover it with your right. Then execute a **left elbow strike** (Hidari te embi) behind you as if striking an opponent's chin.

26) Shift into a **right leg shoulder stance** (Migi ashi zenkutsudachi at an angle) to the opposite direction and make a fist with your right hand, covering it with your left. Then execute a **right elbow strike** (Migi te embi) behind you as if striking an opponent's chin.

27) Shift back to a **ready stance** (Uchihachiji dachi) and reach out executing a **collar grab**.

Pull both fists back to tsuki, executing a **double backwards elbow strike** (Morote ushiro embi). **Kiai**.

Yame) Bring the left foot together with the right to an **attention stance** (Musubidachi) and finish.

<u>Students testing for 8<sup>th</sup> kyu yellow belt must know the form Ni Ju Shichi No Kata.</u>

**Ni Ju Shichi No Kata: 27 Movements**
**Counts:**
1) **Upper block** with left hand (Hidari te jodan uke).
2) **Upper block** with right hand (Migi te jodan uke).
3) **Outside center block** with left hand (Hidari te chuudan soto uke).
4) **Outside center block** with right hand (Migi te chuudan soto uke).
5) **Inside center block** with left hand (Hidari te chuudan uchi uke).
6) **Inside center block** with right hand (Migi te chuudan uchi uke).
7) **Down block** with left hand (Hidari te gedan uke).
8) **Down block** with right hand (Migi te gedan uke).
9) **Center punch** with left hand (Hidari te chuudan zuki). **Kiai.**
10) **Center punch** with right hand (Migi te chuudan zuki). **Kiai.**
11) Right hand to tsuki position, left hand **punching to the right side** (Hidari te chuudan zuki). Look 45° to the right.
12) Left hand to tsuki position, right hand **punching to the left side** (Migi te chuudan zuki). Look 45° to the left.
13) **Punch over right shoulder** with left fist and a simultaneous **elbow strike** with right elbow (Migi te embi). Look over your right shoulder.
14) **Punch over left shoulder** with right fist and a simultaneous **elbow strike** with left elbow (Hidari te embi). Look over your left shoulder.
15) **Elbow strike** with left elbow to the chin (Hidari te embi).
16) **Elbow strike** with right elbow to the chin (Migi te embi).
17) **Outward knife hand strike** with left hand to temple (Hidari te jodan soto shuto).
18) **Outward knife hand strike** with right hand to temple (Migi te jodan soto shuto).
19) **Upper palm heel strike** with left hand (Hidari te jodan shotei). **Kiai.**
20) **Upper palm heel strike** with right hand (Migi te jodan shotei). **Kiai.**
21) Leaving right hand out, pull left arm horizontal in front of body and then execute an **elbow strike** to the left (Hidari te embi), drawing right hand back to tsuki. Look to the left.
22) Look straight ahead, reach out towards the front with right hand, twist into a **right leg shoulder stance** (Migi ashi zenkutsudachi at an angle) and execute a **left elbow strike** into your right hand (Hidari te embi).
23) Shifting back to a **ready stance** (Uchihachiji dachi), stack left arm on top of right arm and execute an **elbow strike** to the right (Migi te embi), drawing left hand back to tsuki. Look to the right.
24) Look straight ahead, reach out towards the front with your left hand, twist into a **left leg shoulder stance** (Hidari ashi zenkutsudachi at an angle) and execute a **right elbow strike** into your left hand (Migi te embi).
25) Staying in a **left leg shoulder stance** (Hidari ashi zenkutsudachi at an angle), make a fist with your left hand and cover it with your right. Then execute a **left elbow strike** (Hidari te embi) behind you as if striking an opponent's chin.
26) Shift into a **right leg shoulder stance** (Migi ashi zenkutsudachi at an angle) to the opposite direction and make a fist with your right hand, covering it with your left. Then execute a **right elbow strike** (Migi te embi) behind you as if striking an opponent's chin.
27) Shift back to a **ready stance** (Uchihachiji dachi) and reach out executing a **collar grab** and pull both fists back to tsuki, executing a **double backwards elbow strike** (Morote ushiro embi). **Kiai.**

# Kihon Kata Shodan

# First Basic Form

Start from the **ready stance** (Uchihachiji dachi – at position A).

1) Slide left foot in to meet right foot. Then step out to the left (turning 90º towards B) with left foot into a **left foot forward front stance** (Hidari ashi zenkutsudachi). Execute a **left inside center block** (Hidari te chuudan uchi uke).

2) Step forward with right foot into a **right foot forward front stance** (Migi ashi zenkutsudachi). Execute a **right center punch** (Migi te chuudan jun zuki).

3) Turn 180˚ (towards C) with right foot landing in a **right foot forward front stance** (Migi ashi zenkutsudachi). Execute a **right inside center block** (Migi te chuudan uchi uke).

4) Step forward with left foot into a **left foot forward front stance** (Hidari ashi zenkutsudachi). Execute a **left center punch** (Hidari te chuudan jun zuki).

5) Stepping with left foot, turn 90˚ (towards D) landing in a **left foot forward front stance** (Hidari ashi zenkutsudachi). Execute a **left inside center block** (Hidari te chuudan uchi uke).

6) Step forward with right foot into a **right foot forward front stance** (Migi ashi zenkutsudachi). Execute a **right center punch** (Migi te chuudan jun zuki).

7) Step forward with left foot into a **left foot forward front stance** (Hidari ashi zenkutsudachi). Execute a **left center punch** (Hidari te chuudan jun zuki).

8) Step forward with right foot into a **right foot forward front stance** (Migi ashi zenkutsudachi). Execute a **right center punch** (Migi te chuudan jun zuki).

9) Turn 270° (towards E) with left foot landing in a **left foot forward front stance** (Hidari ashi zenkutsudachi). Execute a **left inside center block** (Hidari te chuudan uchi uke).

10) Step forward with right foot into a **right foot forward front stance** (Migi ashi zenkutsudachi). Execute a **right center punch** (Migi te chuudan jun zuki). **Kiai**.

11) Turn 180° (back towards D & F) with right foot and land in a **right foot forward front stance** (Migi ashi zenkutsudachi). Execute a **right inside center block** (Migi te chuudan uchi uke).

12) Step forward with left foot into a **left foot forward front stance** (Hidari ashi zenkutsudachi). Execute a **left center punch** (Hidari te chuudan jun zuki). **Kiai**.

13) Turn 90° (towards A) with left foot and land in a **left foot forward front stance** (Hidari ashi zenkutsudachi). Execute a **left inside center block** (Hidari te chuudan uchi uke).

Execute a **right center reverse punch** (Migi te chuudan gyaku zuki).

**Reverse view**

**Reverse view**

14) Step forward with right foot into a **right foot forward front stance** (Migi ashi zenkutsudachi). Execute a **right inside center block** (Migi te chuudan uchi uke).

Execute a **left center reverse punch** (Hidari te chuudan gyaku zuki).

**Reverse view**

**Reverse view**

15) Step forward with left foot into a **left foot forward front stance** (Hidari ashi zenkutsudachi). Execute a **left inside center block** (Hidari te chuudan uchi uke).

Execute a **right center reverse punch** (Migi te chuudan gyaku zuki).

16) Step forward with right foot into a **right foot forward front stance** (Migi ashi zenkutsudachi). Execute a **right inside center block** (Migi te chuudan uchi uke).

Execute a **left center reverse punch** (Hidari te chuudan gyaku zuki).

17) Turn 270° (towards B) with left foot and land in a **left foot forward front stance** (Hidari ashi zenkutsudachi). Execute a **left inside center block** (Hidari te chuudan uchi uke).

18) Step forward with right foot into a **right foot forward front stance** (Migi ashi zenkutsudachi) and execute a **right center punch** (Migi te chuudan jun zuki). **Kiai**.

19) Turn 180° (back towards A and C) with right foot and land in a **right foot forward front stance** (Migi ashi zenkutsudachi). Execute a **right inside center block** (Migi te chuudan uchi uke).

20) Step forward with left foot into a **left foot forward front stance** (Hidari ashi zenkutsudachi) and execute a **left center punch** (Hidari te chuudan jun zuki). **Kiai.**

21) Shift to a **right one-legged stance** (Migi ashi ippon ashidachi). Execute a **right upper knife hand block** (Migi te jodan shuto uke) while leaving your left arm straight out.

Side view

Shoot your left leg back into a **left leg shoulder stance** (Hidari ashi zenkutsudachi at an angle). Shift to the left and execute a **right lower palm heel block** (Migi te gedan shotei uke). **Kiai.**

Shift into a **right leg shoulder stance** (Migi ashi zenkutsudachi at an angle); execute a **left shoulder punch** (Hidari te kata zuki).

Yame) Bring the left foot together with the right to an **attention stance** (Musubidachi) and finish.

Students testing for 8th kyu yellow belt must know the form Kihon Kata Shodan.

**Kihon Kata Shodan: First Basic Form**

**Counts:**

1) Starting from the **ready stance** (Uchihachiji dachi – at position A), slide left foot in to meet right foot. Then step out to the left (turning 90˚ towards B) with left foot into a **left foot forward front stance** (Hidari ashi zenkutsudachi). Execute a **left inside center block** (Hidari te chuudan uchi uke).

2) Step forward with right foot into a **right foot forward front stance** (Migi ashi zenkutsudachi). Execute a **right center punch** (Migi te chuudan jun zuki).

3) Turn 180˚ (towards C) with right foot landing in a **right foot forward front stance** (Migi ashi zenkutsudachi). Execute a **right inside center block** (Migi te chuudan uchi uke).

4) Step forward with left foot into a **left foot forward front stance** (Hidari ashi zenkutsudachi). Execute a **left center punch** (Hidari te chuudan jun zuki).

5) Stepping with left foot, turn 90˚ (towards D) landing in a **left foot forward front stance** (Hidari ashi zenkutsudachi). Execute a **left inside center block** (Hidari te chuudan uchi uke).

6) Step forward with right foot into a **right foot forward front stance** (Migi ashi zenkutsudachi). Execute a **right center punch** (Migi te chuudan jun zuki).

7) Step forward with left foot into a **left foot forward front stance** (Hidari ashi zenkutsudachi). Execute a **left center punch** (Hidari te chuudan jun zuki).

8) Step forward with right foot into a **right foot forward front stance** (Migi ashi zenkutsudachi). Execute a **right center punch** (Migi te chuudan jun zuki).

9) Turn 270˚ (towards E) with left foot landing in a **left foot forward front stance** (Hidari ashi zenkutsudachi). Execute a **left inside center block** (Hidari te chuudan uchi uke).

10) Step forward with right foot into a **right foot forward front stance** (Migi ashi zenkutsudachi). Execute a **right center punch** (Migi te chuudan jun zuki). **Kiai.**

11) Turn 180˚ (back towards D & F) with right foot and land in a **right foot forward front stance** (Migi ashi zenkutsudachi). Execute a **right inside center block** (Migi te chuudan uchi uke).

12) Step forward with left foot into a **left foot forward front stance** (Hidari ashi zenkutsudachi). Execute a **left center punch** (Hidari te chuudan jun zuki). **Kiai.**

13) Turn 90˚ (towards A) with left foot and land in a **left foot forward front stance** (Hidari ashi zenkutsudachi). Execute a **left inside center block** (Hidari te chuudan uchi uke), and a **right center reverse punch** (Migi te chuudan gyaku zuki).

14) Step forward with right foot into a **right foot forward front stance** (Migi ashi zenkutsudachi). Execute a **right inside center block** (Migi te chuudan uchi uke), and a **left center reverse punch** (Hidari te chuudan gyaku zuki).

15) Step forward with left foot into a **left foot forward front stance** (Hidari ashi zenkutsudachi). Execute a **left inside center block** (Hidari te chuudan uchi uke), and a **right center reverse punch** (Migi te chuudan gyaku zuki).

16) Step forward with right foot into a **right foot forward front stance** (Migi ashi zenkutsudachi). Execute a **right inside center block** (Migi te chuudan uchi uke) and a **left center reverse punch** (Hidari te chuudan gyaku zuki).

17) Turn 270˚ (towards B) with left foot and land in a **left foot forward front stance** (Hidari ashi zenkutsudachi). Execute a **left inside center block** (Hidari te chuudan uchi uke).

18) Step forward with right foot into a **right foot forward front stance** (Migi ashi zenkutsudachi). Execute a **right center punch** (Migi te chuudan jun zuki). **Kiai.**

19) Turn 180° (back towards A and C) with right foot and land in a **right foot forward front stance** (Migi ashi zenkutsudachi). Execute a **right inside center block** (Migi te chuudan uchi uke).

20) Step forward with left foot into a **left foot forward front stance** (Hidari ashi zenkutsudachi). Execute a **left center punch** (Hidari te chuudan jun zuki). **Kiai**.

21) Shift to a **right one-legged stance** (Migi ashi ippon ashidachi). Execute a **right upper knife hand block** (Migi te jodan shuto uke) while leaving your left arm straight out. Shoot your left leg back into a **left leg shoulder stance** (Hidari ashi zenkutsudachi at an angle). Simultaneously, draw your left arm back to tsuki as you shift to the left and execute a **right lower palm heel block** (Migi te gedan shotei uke) as if to block a front kick. **Kiai**. Then shifting into a **right leg shoulder stance** (Migi ashi zenkutsudachi at an angle), execute a **left shoulder punch** (Hidari te kata zuki).

# Kihon Kata Nidan

# Second Basic Form

Start from the **ready stance** (Uchihachiji dachi – at position A).

1) Slide left foot in to meet right foot. Then step out to the left (turning 90° towards B) with left foot into a **left foot forward front stance** (Hidari ashi zenkutsudachi). Execute a **left upper block** (Hidari te jodan uke).

2) Step forward with right foot into a **right foot forward front stance** (Migi ashi zenkutsudachi). Execute a **right upper punch** (Migi te jodan jun zuki).

3) Turn 180° (towards C) with right foot landing in a **right foot forward front stance** (Migi ashi zenkutsudachi). Execute a **right upper block** (Migi te jodan uke).

4) Step forward with left foot into a **left foot forward front stance** (Hidari ashi zenkutsudachi). Execute a **left upper punch** (Hidari te jodan jun zuki).

5) Stepping with left foot, turn 90° (towards D) landing in a **left foot forward front stance** (Hidari ashi zenkutsudachi). Execute a **left upper block** (Hidari te jodan uke).

6) Step forward with right foot into a **right foot forward front stance** (Migi ashi zenkutsudachi). Execute a **right upper punch** (Migi te jodan jun zuki).

7) Step forward with left foot into a **left foot forward front stance** (Hidari ashi zenkutsudachi). Execute a **left upper punch** (Hidari te jodan jun zuki).

8) Step forward with right foot into a **right foot forward front stance** (Migi ashi zenkutsudachi). Execute a **right upper punch** (Migi te jodan jun zuki).

9) Turn 270° (towards E) with left foot landing in a **left foot forward front stance** (Hidari ashi zenkutsudachi). Execute a **left upper block** (Hidari te jodan uke).

10) Step forward with right foot into a **right foot forward front stance** (Migi ashi zenkutsudachi). Execute a **right upper punch** (Migi te jodan jun zuki). **Kiai**.

11) Turn 180° (back towards D & F) with right foot and land in a **right foot forward front stance** (Migi ashi zenkutsudachi). Execute a **right upper block** (Migi te jodan uke).

12) Step forward with left foot into a **left foot forward front stance** (Hidari ashi zenkutsudachi). Execute a **left upper punch** (Hidari te jodan jun zuki). **Kiai**.

13) Turn 90° (towards A) with left foot and land in a **left foot forward front stance** (Hidari ashi zenkutsudachi). Execute a **left upper block** (Hidari te jodan uke).

Execute a **right upper reverse punch** (Migi te jodan gyaku zuki).

**Reverse view**

**Reverse view**

14) Step forward with right foot into a **right foot forward front stance** (Migi ashi zenkutsudachi). Execute a **right upper block** (Migi te jodan uke).

**Reverse view**

**Reverse view**

Execute a **left upper reverse punch** (Hidari te jodan gyaku zuki).

15) Step forward with left foot into a **left foot forward front stance** (Hidari ashi zenkutsudachi). Execute a **left upper block** (Hidari te jodan uke).

Execute a **right upper reverse punch** (Migi te jodan gyaku zuki).

16) Step forward with right foot into a **right foot forward front stance** (Migi ashi zenkutsudachi). Execute a **right upper block** (Migi te jodan uke).

Execute a **left upper reverse punch** (Hidari te jodan gyaku zuki).

17) Turn 270° (towards B) with left foot and land in a **left foot forward front stance** (Hidari ashi zenkutsudachi). Execute a **left upper block** (Hidari te jodan uke).

18) Step forward with right foot into a **right foot forward front stance** (Migi ashi zenkutsudachi). Execute a **right upper punch** (Migi te jodan jun zuki). **Kiai.**

19) Turn 180° (back towards A and C) with right foot and land in a **right foot forward front stance** (Migi ashi zenkutsudachi). Execute a **right upper block** (Migi te jodan uke).

20) Step forward with left foot into a **left foot forward front stance** (Hidari ashi zenkutsudachi) and execute a **left upper punch** (Hidari te jodan jun zuki). **Kiai**.

21) Shift to a **right one-legged stance** (Migi ashi ippon ashidachi). Execute a **right upper knife hand block** (Migi te jodan shuto uke) while leaving your left arm straight out.

Shoot your left leg back into a **left leg shoulder stance** (Hidari ashi zenkutsudachi at an angle). Shift to the left and execute a **right lower palm heel block** (Migi te gedan shotei uke). **Kiai**.

Shift into a **right leg shoulder stance** (Migi ashi zenkutsudachi at an angle); execute a **left shoulder punch** (Hidari te kata zuki).

Yame) Bring the left foot together with the right to an **attention stance** (Musubidachi) and finish.

Students testing for 7<sup>th</sup> kyu yellow belt must know the form Kihon Kata Nidan.

```
┌─────────────────────────────┐
│  ┌───┐   ┌───┐   ┌───┐       │
│  │ C │───│ A │───│ B │       │
│  └───┘   └───┘   └───┘       │
│            │                 │
│  ┌───┐   ┌───┐   ┌───┐       │
│  │ E │───│ D │───│ F │       │
│  └───┘   └───┘   └───┘       │
└─────────────────────────────┘
```

**Kihon Kata Nidan: Second Basic Form**

**Counts:**

1) Starting from the **ready stance** (Uchihachiji dachi – at position A), slide left foot in to meet right foot. Then step out to the left (turning 90˚ towards B) with left foot into a **left foot forward front stance** (Hidari ashi zenkutsudachi). Execute a **left upper block** (Hidari te jodan uke).

2) Step forward with right foot into a **right foot forward front stance** (Migi ashi zenkutsudachi). Execute a **right upper punch** (Migi te jodan jun zuki).

3) Turn 180˚ (towards C) with right foot landing in a **right foot forward front stance** (Migi ashi zenkutsudachi). Execute a **right upper block** (Migi te jodan uke).

4) Step forward with left foot into a **left foot forward front stance** (Hidari ashi zenkutsudachi). Execute a **left upper punch** (Hidari te jodan jun zuki).

5) Stepping with left foot, turn 90˚ (towards D) landing in a **left foot forward front stance** (Hidari ashi zenkutsudachi). Execute a **left upper block** (Hidari te jodan uke).

6) Step forward with right foot into a **right foot forward front stance** (Migi ashi zenkutsudachi). Execute a **right upper punch** (Migi te jodan jun zuki).

7) Step forward with left foot into a **left foot forward front stance** (Hidari ashi zenkutsudachi). Execute a **left upper punch** (Hidari te jodan jun zuki).

8) Step forward with right foot into a **right foot forward front stance** (Migi ashi zenkutsudachi). Execute a **right upper punch** (Migi te jodan jun zuki).

9) Turn 270˚ (towards E) with left foot landing in a **left foot forward front stance** (Hidari ashi zenkutsudachi). Execute a **left upper block** (Hidari te jodan uke).

10) Step forward with right foot into a **right foot forward front stance** (Migi ashi zenkutsudachi). Execute a **right upper punch** (Migi te jodan jun zuki). **Kiai.**

11) Turn 180˚ (back towards D & F) with right foot and land in a **right foot forward front stance** (Migi ashi zenkutsudachi). Execute a **right upper block** (Migi te jodan uke).

12) Step forward with left foot into a **left foot forward front stance** (Hidari ashi zenkutsudachi). Execute a **left upper punch** (Hidari te jodan jun zuki). **Kiai.**

13) Turn 90˚ (towards A) with left foot and land in a **left foot forward front stance** (Hidari ashi zenkutsudachi). Execute a **left upper block** (Hidari te jodan uke), and a **right upper reverse punch** (Migi te jodan gyaku zuki).

14) Step forward with right foot into a **right foot forward front stance** (Migi ashi zenkutsudachi). Execute a **right upper block** (Migi te jodan uke), and a **left upper reverse punch** (Hidari te jodan gyaku zuki).

15) Step forward with left foot into a **left foot forward front stance** (Hidari ashi zenkutsudachi). Execute a **left upper block** (Hidari te jodan uke), and a **right upper reverse punch** (Migi te jodan gyaku zuki).

16) Step forward with right foot into a **right foot forward front stance** (Migi ashi zenkutsudachi). Execute a **right upper block** (Migi te jodan uke) and a **left upper reverse punch** (Hidari te jodan gyaku zuki).

17) Turn 270˚ (towards B) with left foot and land in a **left foot forward front stance** (Hidari ashi zenkutsudachi). Execute a **left upper block** (Hidari te jodan uke).

18) Step forward with right foot into a **right foot forward front stance** (Migi ashi zenkutsudachi). Execute a **right upper punch** (Migi te jodan jun zuki). **Kiai.**

19) Turn 180˚ (back towards A and C) with right foot and land in a **right foot forward front stance** (Migi ashi zenkutsudachi). Execute a **right upper block** (Migi te jodan uke).

20) Step forward with left foot into a **left foot forward front stance** (Hidari ashi zenkutsudachi). Execute a **left upper punch** (Hidari te jodan jun zuki).  **Kiai**.

21) Shift to a **right one-legged stance** (Migi ashi ippon ashidachi).  Execute a **right upper knife hand block** (Migi te jodan shuto uke) while leaving your left arm straight out.  Shoot your left leg back into a **left leg shoulder stance** (Hidari ashi zenkutsudachi at an angle). Simultaneously, draw your left arm back to tsuki as you shift to the left and execute a **right lower palm heel block** (Migi te gedan shotei uke) as if to block a front kick.  **Kiai**.  Then shifting into a **right leg shoulder stance** (Migi ashi zenkutsudachi at an angle), execute a **left shoulder punch** (Hidari te kata zuki).

# Kihon Kata Sandan

# Third Basic Form

Start from the **ready stance** (Uchihachiji dachi – at position A).

1) Slide left foot in to meet right foot, chamber for **down block** with left arm and guard body with right.

Then step out to the left (turning 90° towards B) with left foot into a **left foot forward defensive straddle stance** (Hidari ashi boubi shikodachi). Execute a **left down block** (Hidari te gedan uke).

2) As you begin to move your right foot, lift the left arm to horizontal.

Step forward with right foot into a **right foot forward offensive straddle stance** (Migi ashi kougeki shikodachi). Execute a **right shoulder punch** (Migi te kata zuki).

3) Turn 180° (towards C) with right foot landing in a **right foot forward defensive straddle stance** (Migi ashi boubi shikodachi). Execute a **right down block** (Migi te gedan uke).

4) Step forward with left foot into a **left foot forward offensive straddle stance** (Hidari ashi kougeki shikodachi). Execute a **left shoulder punch** (Hidari te kata zuki).

5) Stepping with left foot, turn 90° (towards D) landing in a **left foot forward defensive straddle stance** (Hidari ashi boubi shikodachi). Execute a **left down block** (Hidari te gedan uke).

6) Step forward with right foot into a **right foot forward offensive straddle stance** (Migi ashi kougeki shikodachi). Execute a **right shoulder punch** (Migi te kata zuki).

Kihon Kata Sandan

7) Step forward with left foot into a **left foot forward offensive straddle stance** (Hidari ashi kougeki shikodachi). Execute a **left shoulder punch** (Hidari te kata zuki).

8) Step forward with right foot into a **right foot forward offensive straddle stance** (Migi ashi kougeki shikodachi). Execute a **right shoulder punch** (Migi te kata zuki).

9) Turn 270° (towards E) with left foot landing in a **left foot forward defensive straddle stance** (Hidari ashi boubi shikodachi). Execute a **left down block** (Hidari te gedan uke).

10) Step forward with right foot into a **right foot forward offensive straddle stance** (Migi ashi kougeki shikodachi). Execute a **right shoulder punch** (Migi te kata zuki). **Kiai.**

11) Turn 180° (back towards D & F) with right foot and land in a **right foot forward defensive straddle stance** (Migi ashi boubi shikodachi). Execute a **right down block** (Migi te gedan uke).

12) Step forward with left foot into a **left foot forward offensive shikodachi stance** (Hidari ashi kougeki shikodachi). Execute a **left shoulder punch** (Hidari te kata zuki). **Kiai.**

13) Turn 90° (towards A) with left foot and land in a **left foot forward defensive straddle stance** (Hidari ashi boubi shikodachi). Execute a **left down block** (Hidari te gedan uke).

Shift into a **left foot forward front stance** (Hidari ashi zenkutsudachi) and execute a **right center reverse punch** (Migi te chuudan gyaku zuki).

**Reverse view**

**Reverse view**

14) Step forward with right foot into a **right foot forward defensive straddle stance** (Migi ashi boubi shikodachi). Execute a **right down block** (Migi te gedan uke).

Shift into a **right foot forward front stance** (Migi ashi zenkutsudachi) and execute a **left center reverse punch** (Hidari te chuudan gyaku zuki).

15) Step forward with left foot into a **left foot forward defensive straddle stance** (Hidari ashi boubi shikodachi). Execute a **left down block** (Hidari te gedan uke).

Shift into a **left foot forward front stance** (Hidari ashi zenkutsudachi) and execute a **right center reverse punch** (Migi te chuudan gyaku zuki).

16) Step forward with right foot into a **right foot forward defensive stance** (Migi ashi boubi shikodachi). Execute a **right down block** (Migi te gedan uke).

Shift into a **right foot forward front stance** (Migi ashi zenkutsudachi) and execute a **left center reverse punch** (Hidari te chuudan gyaku zuki).

17) Turn 270° (towards B) with left foot and land in a **left foot forward defensive straddle stance** (Hidari ashi boubi shikodachi). Execute a **left down block** (Hidari te gedan uke).

18) Step forward with right foot into a **right foot forward offensive straddle stance** (Migi ashi kougeki shikodachi) and execute a **right shoulder punch** (Migi te kata zuki). **Kiai.**

Kihon Kata Sandan

19) Turn 180° (back towards A and C) with right foot and land in a **right foot forward defensive straddle stance** (Migi ashi boubi shikodachi). Execute a **right down block** (Migi te gedan uke).

20) Step forward with left foot into a **left foot forward offensive straddle stance** (Hidari ashi kougeki shikodachi) and execute a **left shoulder punch** (Hidari te kata zuki). **Kiai**.

21) Shift to a **right one-legged stance** (Migi ashi ippon ashidachi). Execute a **right upper knife hand block** (Migi te jodan shuto uke) while leaving your left arm straight out.

Shoot your left leg back into a **left leg shoulder stance** (Hidari ashi zenkutsudachi at an angle). Shift to the left and execute a **right lower palm heel block** (Migi te gedan shotei uke). **Kiai**.

Shift into a **right leg shoulder stance** (Migi ashi zenkutsudachi at an angle); execute a **left shoulder punch** (Hidari te kata zuki).

Yame) Bring the left foot together with the right to an **attention stance** (Musubidachi) and finish.

Kihon Kata Sandan

Students testing for 7th kyu yellow belt must
know the form Kihon Kata Sandan.

```
┌──────────────────────────┐
│  ┌─┐      ┌─┐      ┌─┐   │
│  │C│──────│A│──────│B│   │
│  └─┘      └─┘      └─┘   │
│            │             │
│            │             │
│  ┌─┐      ┌─┐      ┌─┐   │
│  │E│──────│D│──────│F│   │
│  └─┘      └─┘      └─┘   │
└──────────────────────────┘
```

**Kihon Kata Sandan: Third Basic Form**

**Counts:**

1) Starting from the **ready stance** (Uchihachiji dachi – at position A), slide left foot in to meet right foot. Then step out to the left (turning 90° towards B) with left foot into a **left foot forward defensive straddle stance** (Hidari ashi boubi shikodachi). Execute a **left down block** (Hidari te gedan uke).

2) Pick left arm up and then step forward with right foot into a **right foot forward offensive straddle stance** (Migi ashi kougeki shikodachi). Execute a **right shoulder punch** (Migi te kata zuki).

3) Turn 180° (towards C) with right foot landing in a **right foot forward defensive straddle stance** (Migi ashi boubi shikodachi). Execute a **right down block** (Migi te gedan uke).

4) Pick up right arm and then step forward with left foot into a **left foot forward offensive straddle stance** (Hidari ashi kougeki shikodachi). Execute a **left shoulder punch** (Hidari te kata zuki).

5) Stepping with left foot, turn 90° (towards D) landing in a **left foot forward defensive straddle stance** (Hidari ashi boubi shikodachi). Execute a **left down block** (Hidari te gedan uke).

6) Pick up left arm and then step forward with right foot into a **right foot forward offensive straddle stance** (Migi ashi kougeki shikodachi). Execute a **right shoulder punch** (Migi te kata zuki).

7) Step forward with left foot into a **left foot forward offensive straddle stance** (Hidari ashi kougeki shikodachi). Execute a **left shoulder punch** (Hidari te kata zuki).

8) Step forward with right foot into a **right foot forward offensive straddle stance** (Migi ashi kougeki shikodachi). Execute a **right shoulder punch** (Migi te kata zuki).

9) Turn 270° (towards E) with left foot landing in a **left foot forward defensive straddle stance** (Hidari ashi boubi shikodachi). Execute a **left down block** (Hidari te gedan uke).

10) Pick up left arm and step forward with right foot into a **right foot forward offensive straddle stance** (Migi ashi kougeki shikodachi). Execute a **right shoulder punch** (Migi te kata zuki). **Kiai**.

11) Turn 180° (back towards D & F) with right foot and land in a **right foot forward defensive straddle stance** (Migi ashi boubi shikodachi). Execute a **right down block** (Migi te gedan uke).

12) Pick up right arm and step forward with left foot into a **left foot forward offensive straddle stance** (Hidari ashi kougeki shikodachi). Execute a **left shoulder punch** (Hidari te kata zuki). **Kiai**.

13) Turn 90° (towards A) with left foot and land in a **left foot forward defensive straddle stance** (Hidari ashi boubi shikodachi). Execute a **left down block** (Hidari te gedan uke). Then shift into a **left foot forward front stance** (Hidari ashi zenkutsudachi) and execute a **right center reverse punch** (Migi te chuudan gyaku zuki).

14) Step forward with right foot into a **right foot forward defensive straddle stance** (Migi ashi boubi shikodachi). Execute a **right down block** (Migi te gedan uke). Then shift into a **right foot forward front stance** (Migi ashi zenkutsudachi) and execute a **left center reverse punch** (Hidari te chuudan gyaku zuki).

15) Step forward with left foot into a **left foot forward defensive straddle stance** (Hidari ashi boubi shikodachi).  Execute a **left down block** (Hidari te gedan uke).  Then shift into a **left foot forward front stance** (Hidari ashi zenkutsudachi) and execute a **right center reverse punch** (Migi te chuudan gyaku zuki).

16) Step forward with right foot into a **right foot forward defensive stance** (Migi ashi boubi shikodachi).  Execute a **right down block** (Migi te gedan uke).  Then shift into a **right foot forward front stance** (Migi ashi zenkutsudachi) and execute a **left center reverse punch** (Hidari te chuudan gyaku zuki).

17) Turn 270° (towards B) with left foot and land in a **left foot forward defensive straddle** stance (Hidari ashi boubi shikodachi).  Execute a **left down block** (Hidari te gedan uke).

18) Pick up the left arm and step forward with right foot into a **right foot forward offensive straddle stance** (Migi ashi kougeki shikodachi) and execute a **right shoulder punch** (Migi te kata zuki).  **Kiai**.

19) Turn 180° (back towards A and C) with right foot and land in a **right foot forward defensive straddle stance** (Migi ashi boubi shikodachi).  Execute a **right down block** (Migi te gedan uke).

20) Pick up the right arm and step forward with left foot into a **left foot forward offensive straddle stance** (Hidari ashi kougeki shikodachi) and execute a **left shoulder punch** (Hidari te kata zuki).  **Kiai**.

21) Shift to a **right one-legged stance** (Migi ashi ippon ashidachi).  Execute a **right upper knife hand block** (Migi te jodan shuto uke) while leaving your left arm straight out.  Shoot your left leg back into a **left leg shoulder stance** (Hidari ashi zenkutsudachi at an angle).  Simultaneously, draw your left arm back to tsuki as you shift to the left and execute a **right lower palm heel block** (Migi te gedan shotei uke) as if to block a front kick.  **Kiai**.  Then shifting into a **right leg shoulder stance** (Migi ashi zenkutsudachi at an angle), execute a **left shoulder punch** (Hidari te kata zuki).

# Kihon Kata Yondan

# Fourth Basic Form

Start from the **ready stance** (Uchihachiji dachi – at position A).

1) Step out to the left (turning 90° towards B) with left foot into a **left foot forward defensive straddle stance** (Hidari ashi boubi shikodachi). Execute a **left down block** (Hidari te gedan uke).

2) Chamber for **front kick** with the right foot.

Leaving left arm in down block position, execute a **right front kick** (Migi ashi mae geri).

Land forward into a **right foot forward front stance** (Migi ashi zenkutsudachi).

After landing, execute a **right center punch** (Migi te chuudan jun zuki).

3) Turn 180° (towards C) with right foot landing in a **right foot forward defensive straddle stance** (Migi ashi boubi shikodachi). Execute a **right down block** (Migi te gedan uke).

4) Leaving right arm in down block position, execute a **left front kick** (Hidari ashi mae geri).

Properly recoil all kicks before landing.

Land forward into a **left foot forward front stance** (Hidari ashi zenkutsudachi) and then execute a **left center punch** (Hidari te chuudan jun zuki).

5) Stepping with left foot, turn 90° (towards D) landing in a **left foot forward defensive straddle stance** (Hidari ashi boubi shikodachi). Execute a **left down block** (Hidari te gedan uke).

6) Lift the left arm to horizontal and step forward with right foot into a **right foot forward offensive straddle stance** (Migi ashi kougeki shikodachi). Execute a **right shoulder punch** (Migi te kata zuki).

7) Step forward with left foot into a **left foot forward offensive straddle stance** (Hidari ashi kougeki shikodachi). Execute a **left shoulder punch** (Hidari te kata zuki).

8) Step forward with right foot into a **right foot forward offensive straddle stance** (Migi ashi kougeki shikodachi). Execute a **right shoulder punch** (Migi te kata zuki).

9) Turn 270° (towards E) with left foot landing in a **left foot forward defensive straddle stance** (Hidari ashi boubi shikodachi). Execute a **left down block** (Hidari te gedan uke).

10) Leaving left arm in down block position, execute a **right front kick** (Migi ashi mae geri).

Land forward into a **right foot forward front stance** (Migi ashi zenkutsudachi) and then execute a **right center punch** (Migi te chuudan jun zuki). **Kiai**.

11) Turn 180° (back towards D & F) with right foot and land in a **right foot forward defensive straddle stance** (Migi ashi boubi shikodachi). Execute a **right down block** (Migi te gedan uke).

Kihon Kata Yondan

12) Leaving right arm in down block position, execute a **left front kick** (Hidari ashi mae geri).

Land forward into a **left foot forward front stance** (Hidari ashi zenkutsudachi) and then execute a **left center punch** (Hidari te chuudan jun zuki). **Kiai**.

13) Turn 90° (towards A) with left foot and land in a **left foot forward defensive straddle stance** (Hidari ashi boubi shikodachi). Execute a **left down block** (Hidari te gedan uke).

Shift into a **left foot forward front stance** (Hidari ashi zenkutsudachi) and execute a **right center reverse punch** (Migi te chuudan gyaku zuki).

Step forward into a **right foot forward defensive straddle stance** (Migi ashi boubi shikodachi) and execute a **double knife hand block** (Morote shuto uke) slowly with tension.

**Side view**

**Side view**

**Side view**

Chamber for double knife hand block (Nidan shuto uke).

**Side view**

Kihon Kata Yondan

14) Step forward with left foot into a **left foot forward defensive straddle stance** (Hidari ashi boubi shikodachi). Execute a **left down block** (Hidari te gedan uke).

Shift into a **left foot forward front stance** (Hidari ashi zenkutsudachi) and execute a **right center reverse punch** (Migi te chuudan gyaku zuki).

Step forward into a **right foot forward defensive straddle stance** (Migi ashi boubi shikodachi) and execute a **double knife hand block** (Morote shuto uke) slowly with tension.

15) Turn 270° (towards B) with left foot and land in a **left foot forward defensive straddle stance** (Hidari ashi boubi shikodachi). Execute a **left down block** (Hidari te gedan uke).

16) Leaving left arm in down block position, execute a **right front kick** (Migi ashi mae geri).

Land forward into a **right foot forward front stance** (Migi ashi zenkutsudachi) and then execute a **right center punch** (Migi te chuudan jun zuki). **Kiai.**

17) Turn 180° (back towards A and C) with right foot and land in a **right foot forward defensive straddle stance** (Migi ashi boubi shikodachi). Execute a **right down block** (Migi te gedan uke).

18) Leaving right arm in down block position, execute a **left front kick** (Hidari ashi mae geri).

Land forward into a **left foot forward front stance** (Hidari ashi zenkutsudachi) and then execute a **left center punch** (Hidari te chuudan jun zuki). **Kiai.**

Kihon Kata Yondan

19) Shift to a **right one-legged stance** (Migi ashi ippon ashidachi). Execute a **right upper knife hand block** (Migi te jodan shuto uke) while leaving your left arm straight out.

Shoot your left leg back into a **left leg shoulder stance** (Hidari ashi zenkutsudachi at an angle). Shift to the left and execute a **right lower palm heel block** (Migi te gedan shotei uke). **Kiai.**

Shift into a **right leg shoulder stance** (Migi ashi zenkutsudachi at an angle); execute a **left shoulder punch** (Hidari te kata zuki).

Yame) Bring the left foot together with the right to an **attention stance** (Musubidachi) and finish.

Students testing for 6<sup>th</sup> kyu blue belt must know the form Kihon Kata Yondan.

**Kihon Kata Yondan: Fourth Basic Form**

**Counts:**

1) Starting from the **ready stance** (Uchihachiji dachi – at position A), slide left foot in to meet right foot. Then step out to the left (turning 90˚ towards B) with left foot into a **left foot forward defensive straddle stance** (Hidari ashi boubi shikodachi). Execute a **left down block** (Hidari te gedan uke).

2) Leaving left arm in down block position, execute a **right front kick** (Migi ashi mae geri). Land forward into a **right foot forward front stance** (Migi ashi zenkutsudachi). After landing, execute a **right center punch** (Migi te chuudan jun zuki).

3) Turn 180˚ (towards C) with right foot landing in a **right foot forward defensive straddle stance** (Migi ashi boubi shikodachi). Execute a **right down block** (Migi te gedan uke).

4) Leaving right arm in down block position, execute a **left front kick** (Hidari ashi mae geri). Land forward into a **left foot forward front stance** (Hidari ashi zenkutsudachi) and then execute a **left center punch** (Hidari te chuudan jun zuki).

5) Stepping with left foot, turn 90˚ (towards D) landing in a **left foot forward defensive straddle stance** (Hidari ashi boubi shikodachi). Execute a **left down block** (Hidari te gedan uke).

6) Pick up left arm and then step forward with right foot into a **right foot forward offensive straddle stance** (Migi ashi kougeki shikodachi). Execute a **right shoulder punch** (Migi te kata zuki).

7) Step forward with left foot into a **left foot forward offensive straddle stance** (Hidari ashi kougeki shikodachi). Execute a **left shoulder punch** (Hidari te kata zuki).

8) Step forward with right foot into a **right foot forward offensive straddle stance** (Migi ashi kougeki shikodachi). Execute a **right shoulder punch** (Migi te kata zuki).

9) Turn 270˚ (towards E) with left foot landing in a **left foot forward defensive straddle stance** (Hidari ashi boubi shikodachi). Execute a **left down block** (Hidari te gedan uke).

10) Leaving left arm in down block position, execute a **right front kick** (Migi ashi mae geri). Land forward into a **right foot forward front stance** (Migi ashi zenkutsudachi) and then execute a **right center punch** (Migi te chuudan jun zuki). **Kiai**.

11) Turn 180˚ (back towards D & F) with right foot and land in a **right foot forward defensive straddle stance** (Migi ashi boubi shikodachi). Execute a **right down block** (Migi te gedan uke).

12) Leaving right arm in down block position, execute a **left front kick** (Hidari ashi mae geri). Land forward into a **left foot forward front stance** (Hidari ashi zenkutsudachi) and then execute a **left center punch** (Hidari te chuudan jun zuki). **Kiai**.

13) Turn 90˚ (towards A) with left foot and land in a **left foot forward defensive straddle stance** (Hidari ashi boubi shikodachi). Execute a **left down block** (Hidari te gedan uke). Then shift into a **left foot forward front stance** (Hidari ashi zenkutsudachi) and execute a **right center reverse punch** (Migi te chuudan gyaku zuki). Step forward into a **right foot forward defensive straddle stance** (Migi ashi boubi shikodachi) and execute a **double knife hand block** (Morote shuto uke) slowly with tension.

14) Step forward with left foot into a **left foot forward defensive straddle stance** (Hidari ashi boubi shikodachi). Execute a **left down block** (Hidari te gedan uke). Then shift into a **left foot forward front stance** (Hidari ashi zenkutsudachi) and execute a **right center reverse punch** (Migi te chuudan gyaku zuki). Step forward into a **right foot forward defensive straddle stance** (Migi ashi boubi shikodachi) and execute a **double knife hand block** (Morote shuto uke) slowly with tension.

15) Turn 270° (towards B) with left foot and land in a **left foot forward defensive straddle** stance (Hidari ashi boubi shikodachi). Execute a **left down block** (Hidari te gedan uke).

16) Leaving left arm in down block position, execute a **right front kick** (Migi ashi mae geri). Land forward into a **right foot forward front stance** (Migi ashi zenkutsudachi) and then execute a **right center punch** (Migi te chuudan jun zuki). **Kiai.**

17) Turn 180° (back towards A and C) with right foot and land in a **right foot forward defensive straddle stance** (Migi ashi boubi shikodachi). Execute a **right down block** (Migi te gedan uke).

18) Leaving right arm in down block position, execute a **left front kick** (Hidari ashi mae geri). Land forward into a **left foot forward front stance** (Hidari ashi zenkutsudachi) and then execute a **left center punch** (Hidari te chuudan jun zuki). **Kiai.**

19) Shift to a **right one-legged stance** (Migi ashi ippon ashidachi). Execute a **right upper knife hand block** (Migi te jodan shuto uke) while leaving your left arm straight out. Shoot your left leg back into a **left leg shoulder stance** (Hidari ashi zenkutsudachi at an angle). Simultaneously, draw your left arm back to tsuki as you shift to the left and execute a **right lower palm heel block** (Migi te gedan shotei uke) as if to block a front kick. **Kiai.** Then shifting into a **right leg shoulder stance** (Migi ashi zenkutsudachi at an angle), execute a **left shoulder punch** (Hidari te kata zuki).

# Zenshin Kotai

# Advancing and Retreating

52

Start from the **ready stance** (Uchihachiji dachi – at position A).

1) Pull your fists to your hips (Tsuki).

2) Step forward (towards B) into a **right foot forward front stance** (Migi ashi zenkutsudachi). Execute a **right center punch** (Migi te chuudan jun zuki). **Kiai**.

3) Step forward into a **left foot forward front stance** (Hidari ashi zenkutsudachi). Execute a **left center punch** (Hidari te chuudan jun zuki). **Kiai**.

4) Step back (towards A) into a **right foot forward front stance** (Migi ashi zenkutsudachi). Execute a **right center punch** (Migi te chuudan jun zuki). **Kiai**.

5) Step back into a **left foot forward front stance** (Hidari ashi zenkutsudachi). Execute a **left center punch** (Hidari te chuudan jun zuki). **Kiai**.

6) Slide your right foot in and then out again turning 90° to the right (towards C), chamber for an **inside center block** with the right.

Step forward with the right foot into a **right foot forward front stance** (Migi ashi zenkutsudachi). Execute a **right inside center block** (Migi te chuudan uchi uke) slowly with tension.

Execute a **left center reverse punch** (Hidari te chuudan gyaku zuki).

Zenshin Kotai

Immediately follow with a **right center punch** (Migi te chuudan jun zuki).

7) Slide your left foot in and then out again turning 180° (towards D). Chamber for an **inside center block** with the left.

Step forward with the left foot into a **left foot forward front stance** (Hidari ashi zenkutsudachi). Execute a **left inside center block** (Hidari te chuudan uchi uke) slowly with tension.

Execute a **right center reverse punch** (Migi te chuudan gyaku zuki)

Immediately follow with a **left center punch** (Hidari te chuudan jun zuki).

8) Look to the right, shift into a **left one-legged stance** (Hidari ashi ippon ashidachi) and chamber for a **right down block**, protecting your body with your left arm.

Execute a **right down block** (Migi te gedan uke).

9) Recoil the right hand to tsuki and execute a **right side kick** (Migi ashi yoko geri).

Rechamber the kick correctly, still looking to the right.

Return to a **ready stance** (Uchihachiji dachi) and look to the left. Both hands should now be in tsuki.

10) Shift into a **right one-legged stance** (Migi ashi ippon ashidachi) and chamber for a **left down block**, protecting your body with your right arm.

Execute a **left down block** (Hidari te gedan uke),

11) Recoil left hand to tsuki and execute a **left side kick** (Hidari ashi yoko geri).

Rechamber the kick correctly, now looking forward.

Return to a **ready stance** (Uchihachiji dachi). Both hands should again be in tsuki. Execute a **right center punch** (Migi te chuudan zuki). **Kiai**.

12) Execute a **left center punch** (Hidari te chuudan zuki).

Immediately follow with a **right center punch** (Migi te chuudan zuki)

Immediately follow with a **left center punch** (Hidari te chuudan zuki). **Kiai** on last punch.

Yame) Bring the left foot together with the right to an **attention stance** (Musubidachi) and finish.

Students testing for 6<sup>th</sup> kyu blue belt must know the form Zenshin Kotai.

**Zenshin Kotai: Advancing and Retreating**

**Counts:**
1) Starting from the **ready position**, pull your fists to your hips (Tsuki).
2) Step forward (towards B) into a **right foot forward front stance** (Migi ashi zenkutsudachi). Execute a **right center punch** (Migi te chuudan jun zuki). **Kiai**.
3) Step forward into a **left foot forward front stance** (Hidari ashi zenkutsudachi). Execute a **left center punch** (Hidari te chuudan jun zuki). **Kiai**.
4) Step back (towards A) into a **right foot forward front stance** (Migi ashi zenkutsudachi). Execute a **right center punch** (Migi te chuudan jun zuki). **Kiai**.
5) Step back into a **left foot forward front stance** (Hidari ashi zenkutsudachi). Execute a **left center punch** (Hidari te chuudan jun zuki). **Kiai**.
6) Slide your right foot in and then out again turning 90˚ (towards C) landing in a **right foot forward front stance** (Migi ashi zenkutsudachi). Execute a **right inside center block** (Migi te chuudan uchi uke) slowly with tension. Execute a **left center reverse punch** (Hidari te chuudan gyaku zuki) followed immediately by a **right center punch** (Migi te chuudan jun zuki).
7) Slide your left foot in and then out again turning 180˚ (towards D) landing in a **left foot forward front stance** (Hidari ashi zenkutsudachi). Execute a **left inside center block** (Hidari te chuudan uchi uke) slowly with tension. Execute a **right center reverse punch** (Migi te chuudan gyaku zuki) followed immediately by a **left center punch** (Hidari te chuudan jun zuki).
8) Look to the right, shift into a **left one-legged stance** (Hidari ashi ippon ashidachi) and execute a **right down block** (Migi te gedan uke), being sure to chamber the left hand across the body.
9) Recoil right hand to tsuki and execute a **right side kick** (Migi ashi yoko geri). Return to a **ready stance** (Uchihachiji dachi) and look to the left. Both hands should now be in tsuki.
10) Shift into a **right one-legged stance** (Migi ashi ippon ashidachi) and execute a **left down block** (Hidari te gedan uke), being sure to chamber the right across the body.
11) Recoil left hand to tsuki and execute a **left side kick** (Hidari ashi yoko geri). Return to a **ready stance** (Uchihachiji dachi) and look straight ahead. Both hands should again be in tsuki. Execute a **right center punch** (Migi te chuudan zuki). **Kiai**.
12) Execute a **left center punch** (Hidari te chuudan zuki), immediately followed by a **right center punch** (Migi te chuudan zuki), and immediately followed by a **left center punch** (Hidari te chuudan zuki). **Kiai** on last punch.

# Shihohai

# Four Directions

Start from the **ready stance** (Uchihachiji dachi – at position A).

1) Pull your fists to your hips (Tsuki).

2) Start each count by looking in the direction you will be turning.

Leaving your left foot in place, slide your right foot forward into a **ready stance** (Uchihachiji dachi) turning 90° to your left (towards B). Execute a **right center punch** (Migi te chuudan zuki). **Kiai**.

3) Leaving your right foot in place and holding your right arm out, slide your left foot backwards into a **ready stance** (Uchihachiji dachi) turning 90° to your left (towards C) Execute a **left center punch** (Hidari te chuudan zuki). **Kiai**.

**Reverse view**

4) Leaving your left foot in place and holding your left arm out, slide your right foot forward into a **ready stance** (Uchihachiji dachi) turning 90° to your left (towards D). Execute a **right center punch** (Migi te chuudan zuki). **Kiai**.

5) Leaving your right foot in place and holding your right arm out, slide your left foot backwards into a **ready stance** (Uchihachiji dachi) turning 90° to your left (towards E) so that you are back in your starting position. Execute a **left center punch** (Hidari te chuudan zuki). **Kiai**.

6) Looking to the right and moving your right foot, step back into a **left foot forward scissor stance** (Hidari ashi hasamidachi) with your hips facing the front of the room and simultaneously execute a **right backfist** (towards D) with the wrist bent (Migi te uraken).

Chamber for a **right front kick** and simultaneously turn your hips so they are facing the right (towards C).

Then execute a **right front kick** (Migi ashi mae geri).

Rechamber your kick.

Land forward into a **right foot forward front stance** (Migi ashi zenkutsudachi). Execute a **left center reverse punch** (Hidari te chuudan gyaku zuki).

Immediately follow with a **right center punch** (Migi te chuudan jun zuki).

7) Looking to the left and moving your left foot, step back into **right foot forward scissor stance** (Migi ashi hasamidachi) with your hips facing the front of the room and simultaneously execute a **left backfist** (towards B) with the wrist bent (Hidari te uraken).

Chamber for a **left front kick** and simultaneously turn your hips so they are facing the left (towards D).

Then execute a **left front kick** (Hidari ashi mae geri).

Rechamber your kick.

Land forward into a **left foot forward front stance** (Hidari ashi zenkutsudachi). Execute a **right center reverse punch** (Migi te chuudan gyaku zuki).

Immediately follow with a **left center punch** (Hidari te chuudan jun zuki).

8) Look to the right (towards D), shift into a **left one-legged stance** (Hidari ashi ippon ashidachi) and chamber for a **right down block**, protecting your body with your left arm.

Execute a **right down block** (Migi te gedan uke).

9) Recoil the right hand to tsuki and execute a **right side kick** (Migi ashi yoko geri).

Rechamber the kick correctly, still looking to the right.

Return to a **ready stance** (Uchihachiji dachi) and look to the left (towards B). Both hands should now be in tsuki.

10) Shift into a **right one-legged stance** (Migi ashi ippon ashidachi) and chamber for a **left down block**, protecting your body with your right arm. Execute a **left down block** (Hidari te gedan uke).

11) Recoil left hand to tsuki and execute a **left side kick** (Hidari ashi yoko geri).

Rechamber the kick correctly, now looking forward.

Return to a **ready stance** (Uchihachiji dachi) and look straight ahead (towards E). Both hands should again be in tsuki.

12) Step backward with right foot turning 180° (towards C) into a **right foot forward front stance** (Migi ashi zenkutsudachi) and simultaneously execute a rolling **right backfist** (Migi te uraken) to the bridge of the nose. **Kiai**.

Execute a **left center reverse punch** (Hidari te chuudan gyaku zuki).

Immediately follow with a **right center punch** (Migi te chuudan jun zuki).

13) Step backward with right foot turning 180° (towards E) into a **right foot forward front stance** (Migi ashi zenkutsudachi) and simultaneously execute a rolling **right backfist** (Migi te uraken) to the bridge of the nose. **Kiai**.

Execute a **left center reverse punch** (Hidari te chuudan gyaku zuki).

Immediately follow with a **right center punch** (Migi te chuudan jun zuki).

Yame) Bring the left foot together with the right to an **attention stance** (Musubidachi) and finish.

Students <u>testing for 5<sup>th</sup> kyu blue belt must
know the form Shihohai.</u>

**Shihohai: Four Directions**

**Counts:**
1) Starting from the **ready position**, pull your fists to your hips (Tsuki) (Position A).
2) Leaving your left foot in place, slide your right foot forward into a **ready stance** (Uchihachiji dachi) turning 90˚ to your left (towards B). Execute a **right center punch** (Migi te chuudan zuki). **Kiai**.
3) Leaving your right foot in place and holding your right arm out, slide your left foot backwards into a **ready stance** (Uchihachiji dachi) turning 90˚ so that you are facing opposite your starting position (towards C). Execute a **left center punch** (Hidari te chuudan zuki). **Kiai**.
4) Leaving your left foot in place and holding your left arm out, slide your right foot forward into a **ready stance** (Uchihachiji dachi) turning 90˚ to your left (towards D). Execute a **right center punch** (Migi te chuudan zuki). **Kiai**.
5) Leaving your right foot in place and holding your right arm out, slide your left foot backwards into a **ready stance** (Uchihachiji dachi) turning 90˚ (towards E) so that you are back in your starting position. Execute a **left center punch** (Hidari te chuudan zuki). **Kiai**.
6) Looking to the right and moving your right foot, step back into a **left foot forward scissor stance** (Hidari ashi hasamidachi) with your hips facing the front of the room and simultaneously execute a **right backfist** (targeting towards D) with the wrist bent (Migi te uraken). On the same count, chamber for a **right front kick** and simultaneously turn your hips so they are facing the right. Then execute a **right front kick** (Migi ashi mae geri). Land forward into a **right foot forward front stance** (Migi ashi zenkutsudachi). Execute a **left center reverse punch** (Hidari te chuudan gyaku zuki) and immediately follow with a **right center punch** (Migi te chuudan jun zuki).
7) Looking 180º to the left and moving your left foot, step back into a **right foot forward scissor stance** (Migi ashi hasamidachi) with your hips facing the front of the room and simultaneously execute a **left backfist** (targeting towards B) with the wrist bent (Hidari te uraken). On the same count, chamber for a **left front kick** and simultaneously turn your hips so they are facing the left. Then execute a **left front kick** (Hidari ashi mae geri). Land forward into a **left foot forward front stance** (Hidari ashi zenkutsudachi). Execute a **right center reverse punch** (Migi te chuudan gyaku zuki) and immediately follow with a **left center punch** (Hidari te chuudan jun zuki).
8) Turn 180º to the right (towards D) and shift into a **left one-legged stance** (Hidari ashi ippon ashidachi). Simultaneously execute a **right down block** (Migi te gedan uke), being sure to chamber the left hand across the body.
9) Recoil right hand to tsuki and execute a **right side kick** (Migi ashi yoko geri). Return to a **ready stance** (Uchihachiji dachi) and look to the left (towards B). Both hands should now be in tsuki.
10) Shift into a **right one-legged stance** (Migi ashi ippon ashidachi). Simultaneously execute a **left down block** (Hidari te gedan uke), being sure to chamber the right across the body.
11) Recoil left hand to tsuki and execute a **left side kick** (Hidari ashi yoko geri). Return to a **ready stance** (Uchihachiji dachi) and look straight ahead. Both hands should again be in tsuki.

12) Step backward with right foot turning 180° into a **right foot forward front stance** (Migi ashi zenkutsudachi) (towards C) and simultaneously execute a rolling **right backfist** (Migi te uraken) to the bridge of the nose. **Kiai**. Execute a **left center reverse punch** (Hidari te chuudan gyaku zuki) and immediately follow with a **right center punch** (Migi te chuudan jun zuki).

13) Step backward with right foot turning 180° into a **right foot forward front stance** (Migi ashi zenkutsudachi) (towards E) and simultaneously execute a rolling **right backfist** (Migi te uraken) to the bridge of the nose. **Kiai**. Execute a **left center reverse punch** (Hidari te chuudan gyaku zuki) and immediately follow with a **right center punch** (Migi te chuudan jun zuki).

Shihohai

# Seisan

# Thirteen Hands

Start from the **ready stance** (Uchihachiji dachi – at position A).

1) Moving your left foot, step forward into a **left foot forward front stance** (Hidari ashi zenkutsudachi). Execute a **left inside center block** (Hidari te chuudan uchi uke).

Immediately follow with **a right center reverse punch** (Migi te chuudan gyaku zuki).

With the same hand, without chambering, execute a **right inside center block** (Migi te chuudan uchi uke).

Do the block slowly with tension.

2) Moving your right foot, step forward into a **right foot forward front stance** (Migi ashi zenkutsudachi). As you step forward leave your torso and right arm in the same position.

After landing in your stance, shift your torso and arm to the right to face forward slowly with tension.

3) Execute a **left center reverse punch** (Hidari te chuudan gyaku zuki).

With the same hand, without chambering, execute a **left inside center block** (Hidari te chuudan uchi uke).

Do the block slowly with tension.

4) Moving your left foot, step forward into a **left foot forward front stance** (Hidari ashi zenkutsudachi). As you step forward leave your torso and left arm in the same position.

After landing in your stance, shift your torso and arm to the left to face forward slowly with tension.

5) Execute a **right center reverse punch** (Migi te chuudan gyaku zuki).

With the same hand, without chambering, execute a **right inside center block** (Migi te chuudan uchi uke).

Do the block slowly with tension.

6) Shift back into a **left foot forward defensive straddle stance** (Hidari ashi boubi shikodachi) while simultaneously bringing your right hand back to tsuki and executing a **left upper block** (Hidari te jodan uke).

Slide forward into a **left foot forward transitional stance** and simultaneously execute a **right upper reverse punch** (Migi te jodan gyaku zuki). **Kiai.**

Turning 180° into an **attention stance** (Musubidachi) with knees slightly bent; execute a **double back hand block** (Morote haisho uke) in front of your face. Continue to the next move without pause.

**Reverse view**

Step back with your right foot into a **left foot forward front stance** (Hidari ashi zenkutsudachi). Move both hands down to your sides with your palms down.

**Reverse view**

7) Step forward with your right foot into a **right foot forward front stance** (Migi ashi zenkutsudachi). Bring your right hand up to your chest (near the left axilla) and execute a **right inverted ridge hand block** (Migi te haito uke).

Then turn your right hand over to grab an imaginary wrist. Pull your right hand down slowly towards your hip.

Then move the hand straight out to your right side as if throwing an opponent.

**Reverse view**

**Reverse view**

**Reverse view**

Seisan

**Reverse view**

8) Step forward with your left foot into a **left foot forward front stance** (Hidari ashi zenkutsudachi). Bring your left hand up to your chest (near the right axilla) and execute a **left inverted ridge hand block** (Hidari te haito uke).

Then turn your left hand over to grab an imaginary wrist. Pull your left hand down slowly towards your hip and then straight out to your left side as if throwing an opponent.

**Reverse view**

**Reverse view**

**Reverse view**

9) Step forward with your right foot into a **right foot forward front stance** (Migi ashi zenkutsudachi). Bring your right hand up to your chest (near the left axilla) and execute a **right inverted ridge hand block** (Migi te haito uke).

Then turn your right hand over to grab an imaginary wrist. Pull your right hand down slowly towards your hip, then move the hand straight out to your right side as if throwing an opponent.

10) Moving your right foot, slide back one foot into a **left foot forward front stance** (Hidari ashi zenkutsudachi) turning 90° to your left. Execute a **left inside center block** (Hidari te chuudan uchi uke) slowly with tension.

11) Execute a **right upper reverse punch** (Migi te jodan gyaku zuki).

Shift your stance into a **left foot forward defensive straddle stance** (Hidari ashi boubi shikodachi) and simultaneously execute a **left shoulder punch** (Hidari te kata zuki).

Execute a **right front kick** (Migi ashi mae geri) and set your right foot back into a **left foot forward front stance** (Hidari ashi zenkutsudachi).

Execute a **right center reverse punch** (Migi te chuudan gyaku zuki).

12) Moving your left foot, slide back one foot into a **right foot forward front stance** (Migi ashi zenkutsudachi) turning 180° to your right. Execute a **right inside center block** (Migi te chuudan uchi uke) slowly with tension.

13) Execute a **left upper reverse punch** (Hidari te jodan gyaku zuki),

Shift your stance into a **right foot forward defense straddle stance** (Migi ashi boubi shikodachi) and simultaneously execute a **right shoulder punch** (Migi te kata zuki).

Execute a **left front kick** (Hidari ashi mae geri) and set your left foot back into a **right foot forward front stance** (Migi ashi zenkutsudachi).

Execute a **left center reverse punch** (Hidari te chuudan gyaku zuki).

14) Moving your right foot, slide back one foot into a **left foot forward front stance** turning 90° to your left. Execute a **left inside center block** (Hidari te chuudan uchi uke) slowly with tension.

15) Execute a **right upper reverse punch** (Migi te jodan gyaku zuki).

Shift your stance into a **left foot forward defensive straddle stance** (Hidari ashi boubi shikodachi) and simultaneously execute a **left shoulder punch** (Hidari te kata zuki).

Execute a **right front kick** (Migi ashi mae geri) and set your right foot back into a **left foot forward front stance** (Hidari ashi zenkutsudachi).

Execute a **right center reverse punch** (Migi te chuudan gyaku zuki).

16) Shift into a **left one-legged stance** (Hidari ashi ippon ashidachi) turning 180° with your right arm stacked on top of your left.

Step forward into an **attention stance** (Musubidachi) and execute a **right backfist** (Migi te uraken) to the bridge of the nose. **Kiai**.

**Side view**

Slide backward into a **right foot forward cat stance** (Migi ashi neko ashidachi) and execute a **right elbow block** (Migi te embi uke).

**Side view**

17) Stomp your right heel down on the ground and then step through with your left foot.

Stepping through with left foot

Execute a **right front kick** (Migi ashi mae geri).

Fully recoil all kicks

Land in a **right foot forward defensive straddle stance** (Migi ashi boubi shikodachi) and execute a **right down block** (Migi te gedan uke).

Shift into a **right foot forward front stance** (Migi ashi zenkutsudachi) as you simultaneously execute a **left center reverse punch** (Hidari te chuudan gyaku zuki).

Execute a **right inside center block** (Migi te chuudan uchi uke) slowly with tension.

18) Shift into a **right one-legged stance** (Migi ashi ippon ashidachi) turning 180° with your left arm stacked on top of your right.

Seisan

Step forward into an **attention stance** (Musubidachi) and execute a **left backfist** (Hidari te uraken) to the bridge of the nose. **Kiai**.

Slide backward into a **left foot forward cat stance** (Hidari ashi neko ashidachi) and execute a **left elbow block** (Hidari te embi uke).

19) Stomp your left heel down on the ground and then step through with your right foot.

Execute a **left front kick** (Hidari ashi mae geri).

Land in a **left foot forward defensive straddle stance** (Hidari ashi boubi shikodachi) and execute a **left down block** (Hidari te gedan uke).

Shift into a **left foot forward front stance** (Hidari ashi zenkutsudachi) as you simultaneously execute a **right center reverse punch** (Migi te chuudan gyaku zuki).

Execute a **left inside center block** (Hidari te chuudan uchi uke) slowly with tension.

20) Slide your right foot in to meet your left and then (turning 180º) slide it out into a **right foot forward offensive straddle stance** (Migi ashi kougeki shikodachi) and execute a **right inverted hammer fist** (Migi te tsutsuken) to the floating ribs. **Kiai**.

Slide your left foot up and then slide back into a **right foot forward defensive straddle stance** (Migi ashi boubi shikodachi) and execute a **right down block** (Migi te gedan uke).

Shift into a **right foot forward front stance** (Migi ashi zenkutsudachi) as you simultaneously execute a **left center reverse punch** (Hidari te chuudan gyaku zuki).

Execute a **right inside center block** (Migi te chuudan uchi uke) slowly with tension.

21) Step back with your right foot into a **left foot forward front stance** (Hidari ashi zenkutsudachi) and execute a **left upper knife hand block** (Hidari te jodan shuto uke), settling your hand to the left of center.

22) Leaving your left hand in place, execute a **right front kick** (Migi ashi mae geri).

Land back in a **left foot forward front stance** (Hidari ashi zenkutsudachi). Then execute a **right center reverse punch** (Migi ashi chuudan gyaku zuki) as you recoil your left hand.

Shoot out both hands in a **double center palm heel block** (Morote chuudan shotei uke).

Slide your stance back as you bring your hands to your abdomen, completing the **palm heel block**.

Turn your hands counterclockwise (as if breaking a foot).

Yame) Bring the right foot together with the left to an **attention stance** (Musubidachi) and finish.

Students testing for 4<sup>th</sup> kyu green belt must
know the form Seisan.

**Seisan: Thirteen Hands**

**Counts:**

1) Start from the **ready stance** (Uchihachiji dachi – at position A). Moving your left foot, step forward into a **left foot forward front stance** (Hidari ashi zenkutsudachi). Execute a **left inside center block** (Hidari te chuudan uchi uke). Immediately follow with **a right center reverse punch** (Migi te chuudan gyaku zuki). With the same hand, without chambering, execute a **right inside center block** (Migi te chuudan uchi uke). Do the block slowly with tension.

2) Moving your right foot, step forward into a **right foot forward front stance** (Migi ashi zenkutsudachi). As you step forward leave your torso and right arm in the same position. After landing in your stance, shift your torso and arm to the right to face forward slowly with tension.

3) Execute a **left center reverse punch** (Hidari te chuudan gyaku zuki). With the same hand, without chambering, execute a **left inside center block** (Hidari te chuudan uchi uke). Do the block slowly with tension.

4) Moving your left foot, step forward into a **left foot forward front stance** (Hidari ashi zenkutsudachi). As you step forward leave your torso and left arm in the same position. After landing in your stance, shift your torso and arm to the left to face forward slowly with tension.

5) Execute a **right center reverse punch** (Migi te chuudan gyaku zuki). With the same hand, without chambering, execute a **right inside center block** (Migi te chuudan uchi uke). Do the block slowly with tension.

6) Shift back into a **left foot forward defensive straddle stance** (Hidari ashi boubi shikodachi) while simultaneously bringing your right hand back to tsuki and executing a **left upper block** (Hidari te jodan uke). Slide forward into a **left foot forward transitional stance** and simultaneously execute a **right upper reverse punch** (Migi te jodan gyaku zuki). **Kiai**. Turning 180° into an **attention stance** (Musubidachi) with knees slightly bent; execute a **double back hand block** (Morote haisho uke) in front of your face. Step back with your right foot into a **left foot forward front stance** (Hidari ashi zenkutsudachi). Move both hands down to your sides with your palms down.

7) Step forward with your right foot into a **right foot forward front stance** (Migi ashi zenkutsudachi). Bring your right hand up to your chest (near the left axilla) and execute a **right inverted ridge hand block** (Migi te haito uke). Then turn your right hand over to grab an imaginary wrist. Pull your right hand down slowly towards your hip and then straight out to your right side as if throwing an opponent.

8) Step forward with your left foot into a **left foot forward front stance** (Hidari ashi zenkutsudachi). Bring your left hand up to your chest (near the right axilla) and execute a **left inverted ridge hand block** (Hidari te haito uke). Then turn your left hand over to grab an imaginary wrist. Pull your left hand down slowly towards your hip and then straight out to your left side as if throwing an opponent.

9) Step forward with your right foot into a **right foot forward front stance** (Migi ashi zenkutsudachi). Bring your right hand up to your chest (near the left axilla) and execute a **right inverted ridge hand block** (Migi te haito uke). Then turn your right hand over to grab an imaginary wrist. Pull your right hand down slowly towards your hip and then straight out to your right side as if throwing an opponent.

10) Moving your right foot, shift into a **left foot forward front stance** (Hidari ashi zenkutsudachi) turning 90° to your left. Execute a **left inside center block** (Hidari te chuudan uchi uke) slowly with tension.

11) Execute a **right upper reverse punch** (Migi te jodan gyaku zuki). Shift your stance into a **left foot forward defensive straddle stance** (Hidari ashi boubi shikodachi) and simultaneously execute a **left shoulder punch** (Hidari te kata zuki). Execute a **right front kick** (Migi ashi mae geri) and set your right foot back into a **left foot forward front stance** (Hidari ashi zenkutsudachi). Execute a **right center reverse punch** (Migi te chuudan gyaku zuki).

12) Moving your left foot, shift into a **right foot forward front stance** (Migi ashi zenkutsudachi) turning 180° to your right. Execute a **right inside center block** (Migi te chuudan uchi uke) slowly with tension.

13) Execute a **left upper reverse punch** (Hidari te jodan gyaku zuki). Shift your stance into a **right foot forward defense straddle stance** (Migi ashi boubi shikodachi) and simultaneously execute a **right shoulder punch** (Migi te kata zuki). Execute a **left front kick** (Hidari ashi mae geri) and set your left foot back into a **right foot forward front stance** (Migi ashi zenkutsudachi). Execute a **left center reverse punch** (Hidari te chuudan gyaku zuki).

14) Moving your right foot, shift into a **left foot forward front stance** (Hidari ashi zenkutsudachi) turning 90° to your left. Execute a **left inside center block** (Hidari te chuudan uchi uke) slowly with tension.

15) Execute a **right upper reverse punch** (Migi te jodan gyaku zuki). Shift your stance into a **left foot forward defensive straddle stance** (Hidari ashi boubi shikodachi) and simultaneously execute a **left shoulder punch** (Hidari te kata zuki). Execute a **right front kick** (Migi ashi mae geri) and set your right foot back into a **left foot forward front stance** (Hidari ashi zenkutsudachi). Execute a **right center reverse punch** (Migi te chuudan gyaku zuki).

16) Shift into a **left one-legged stance** (Hidari ashi ippon ashidachi) turning 180° with your right arm stacked on top of your left. Step forward into an **attention stance** (Musubidachi) and execute a **right backfist** (Migi te uraken) to the bridge of the nose. **Kiai**. Slide backward into a **right foot forward cat stance** (Migi ashi neko ashidachi) and execute a **right elbow block** (Migi te embi uke).

17) Stomp your right heel down on the ground and then step through with your left foot. Execute a **right front kick** (Migi ashi mae geri). Land in a **right foot forward defensive straddle stance** (Migi ashi boubi shikodachi) and execute a **right down block** (Migi te gedan uke). Shift into a **right foot forward front stance** (Migi ashi zenkutsudachi) as you simultaneously execute a **left center reverse punch** (Hidari te chuudan gyaku zuki). Execute a **right inside center block** (Migi te chuudan uchi uke) slowly with tension.

18) Shift into a **right one-legged stance** (Migi ashi ippon ashidachi) turning 180° with your left arm stacked on top of your right. Step forward into an **attention stance**

(Musubidachi) and execute a **left backfist** (Hidari te uraken) to the bridge of the nose. **Kiai**. Slide backward into a **left foot forward cat stance** (Hidari ashi neko ashidachi) and execute a **left elbow block** (Hidari te embi uke).

19) Stomp your left heel down on the ground and then step through with your right foot. Execute a **left front kick** (Hidari ashi mae geri). Land in a **left foot forward defensive straddle stance** (Hidari ashi boubi shikodachi) and execute a **left down block** (Hidari te gedan uke). Shift into a **left foot forward front stance** (Hidari ashi zenkutsudachi) as you simultaneously execute a **right center reverse punch** (Migi te chuudan gyaku zuki). Execute a **left inside center block** (Hidari te chuudan uchi uke) slowly with tension.

20) Slide your right foot in to meet your left and then (turning 180º) slide it out into a **right foot forward offensive straddle stance** (Migi ashi kougeki shikodachi) and execute a **right inverted hammer fist** (Migi te tsutsuken) to the floating ribs. **Kiai**. Slide your left foot up and then slide back into a **right foot forward defensive straddle stance** (Migi ashi boubi shikodachi) and execute a **right down block** (Migi te gedan uke). Shift into a **right foot forward front stance** (Migi ashi zenkutsudachi) as you simultaneously execute a **left center reverse punch** (Hidari te chuudan gyaku zuki). Execute a **right inside center block** (Migi te chuudan uchi uke) slowly with tension.

21) Step back with your right foot into a **left foot forward front stance** (Hidari ashi zenkutsudachi) and execute a **left upper knife hand block** (Hidari te jodan shuto uke), settling your hand to the left of center.

22) Leaving your left hand in place, execute a **right front kick** (Migi ashi mae geri). Land back in a **left foot forward front stance** (Hidari ashi zenkutsudachi). Then execute a **right center reverse punch** (Migi te chuudan gyaku zuki) as you recoil your left hand. Shoot out both hands in a **double center palm heel block** (Morote chuudan shotei uke). Slide your stance back as you bring your hands to your abdomen, completing the **palm heel block**. Turn your hands counterclockwise (as if breaking a foot).

# Niseishi

# Twenty-Four Steps

Start from the **ready stance** (Uchihachiji dachi – at position A).

1) From **yoi**, execute a **double inside center block** (Morote chuudan uchi uke) with your right arm on the outside, slowly with tension.

2) Step forward with your right foot into a **right foot forward front stance** (Migi ashi zenkutsudachi).

Pull hands to **fist to hip position** (Tsuki).

Execute a **double center punch** (Morote chuudan zuki), slowly with tension.

3) Moving your left foot, step up into a **ready stance** (Uchihachiji dachi) and execute a **double inside center block** (Morote chuudan uchi uke) with your left arm on the outside, slowly with tension.

4) Step forward with your right foot into a **right foot forward front stance** (Migi ashi zenkutsudachi), pull hands to **fist to hip position** (Tsuki), then execute a **double center punch** (Morote chuudan zuki), slowly with tension.

5) Pull your left had back to **fist to hip position** (Tsuki).

6) Step forward with your left foot into a **left foot forward front stance** (Hidari ashi zenkutsudachi) and execute a **left center punch** (Hidari te chuudan jun zuki).

Then execute a **right center reverse punch** (Migi te chuudan gyaku zuki).

Slide your right foot in and then out (turning 180°) into a **right foot forward offensive straddle stance** (Migi ashi kougeki shikodachi) as you simultaneously stack your right hand on top of your left.

Execute an **upper right backfist** (Jodan migi te uraken) arcing down to strike the opponent's nose. **Kiai**.

**Side view**

7) Slide your left foot in and then out (turning 180°) into a **left foot forward front stance** (Hidari ashi zenkutsudachi).

Simultaneously swing your right arm around to the front.

Execute a **left center punch** (Hidari te chuudan jun zuki).

Execute a **right center reverse punch** (Migi te chuudan gyaku zuki).

8) Bring your right hand up to your head and chamber your left hand across your chest, guarding the axilla. Both hands should be open with palms facing outward.

Shift into a **left foot forward scissor stance** (Hidari ashi hasamidachi) as you simultaneously execute a **left upper knife hand** (Hidari te jodan shuto) and a **right upper backhand block** (Migi te jodan haisho uke).

**Side view**

Execute a **right front kick** (Migi ashi mae geri).

Land forward and step into a **right foot forward scissor stance** (Migi ashi hasamidachi) as you simultaneously execute a fast **right knife hand block** (Migi te shuto uke).

Execute a fast **left knife hand block** (Hidari te shuto uke).

Leaving the left hand in place, execute a second **right knife hand block** (Migi te shuto uke) slowly with tension to form a **lower backhand cross block** (Gedan haisho juji uke).

9) Moving your left foot back, step into a **right foot forward offensive straddle stance** (Migi ashi kougeki shikodachi). Simultaneously, bring your hands over your head in a circular motion, keeping them crossed.

Chamber your hands to your left shoulder.

Execute a **right inverted ridge hand** (Migi te haito) to the axilla.

**Side view**

Look 180° and bring your right hand up to your head to chamber for a **knife hand**.

Turn 180° into a **left foot forward scissor stance** (Hidari ashi hasamidachi) as you simultaneously execute a **right upper knife hand** (Migi te jodan shuto).

Execute a **right front kick** (Migi ashi mae geri).

Land forward and step into a **right foot forward scissor stance** (Migi ashi hasamidachi) as you simultaneously execute a fast **right knife hand block** (Migi te shuto uke).

Execute a fast **left knife hand block** (Hidari te shuto uke).

Leaving the left hand in place, execute a second **right knife hand block** (Migi te shuto uke) slowly with tension to form a **lower backhand cross block** (Gedan haisho juji uke).

10) Moving your left foot back, step into a **right foot forward offensive straddle stance** (Migi ashi kougeki shikodachi). Simultaneously, bring your hands over your head in a circular motion, keeping them crossed.

Chamber your hands to your left shoulder.

Execute a **right inverted ridge hand** (Migi te haito) to the axilla.

Look 180° and bring your right hand up to your head to chamber for a **knife hand**.

Turn 180° into a **left foot forward scissor stance** (Hidari ashi hasamidachi) as you simultaneously execute a **right upper knife hand** (Migi te jodan shuto).

11) Step up into an **attention stance** (Musubidachi) and bring your right hand into an **upper backhand block** (Migi te jodan haisho uke) in front of your face.

Slowly rotate your arm out to your right and execute a **right upper backhand block** (Migi te jodan haisho uke).

Yame) Finish by remaining in an **attention stance** (Musubidachi) and bringing the hands together as if for **yoi**.

Bring the hands down to groin level as usual for **yoi**, then bow.

Students testing for 2<sup>nd</sup> kyu brown belt must
know the form Niseishi.

**Niseishi: Twenty-Four Steps**

**Counts:**
1) From the **ready position** (Uchihachiji dachi), execute a **double inside center block** (Morote chuudan uchi uke) with your right arm on the outside, slowly with tension.
2) Step forward with your right foot into a **right foot forward front stance** (Migi ashi zenkutsudachi). Pull hands to **fist to hip position** (Tsuki). Execute a **double center punch** (Morote chuudan zuki) slowly with tension.
3) Moving your left foot, step up into a **ready stance** (Uchihachiji dachi) and execute a **double inside center block** (Morote chuudan uchi uke) with your left arm on the outside, slowly with tension.
4) Step forward with your right foot into a **right foot forward front stance** (Migi ashi zenkutsudachi), pull hands to **fist to hip position** (Tsuki), then execute a **double center punch** (Morote chuudan zuki) slowly with tension.
5) Pull your left had back to **fist to hip position** (Tsuki).
6) Step forward with left foot into a **left foot forward front stance** (Hidari ashi zenkutsudachi) and execute a **left center punch** (Hidari te chuudan jun zuki). Then execute a **right center reverse punch** (Migi te chuudan gyaku zuki). Slide your right foot in and then out (turning 180°) into a **right foot forward offensive straddle stance** (Migi ashi kougeki shikodachi) as you simultaneously stack your right hand on top of your left. Execute a **right backfist** (Migi te uraken) with your fist turned at approximately 45° such that the striking surface is your first knuckle. **Kiai**.
7) Slide your left foot in and then out (turning 180°) into a **left foot forward front stance** (Hidari ashi zenkutsudachi). Simultaneously, swing your right arm around to the front. Execute a **left center punch** (Hidari te chuudan jun zuki). Execute a **right center reverse punch** (Migi te chuudan gyaku zuki).
8) Bring your right hand up to your head and chamber your left hand across your chest, guarding the axilla. Both hands should be open with palms facing outward. Shift into a **left foot forward scissor stance** (Hidari ashi hasamidachi) as you simultaneously execute a **left upper knife hand** (Hidari te jodan shuto) and a **right upper backhand block** (Migi te jodan haisho uke). Execute a **right front kick** (Migi ashi mae geri). Land forward and step into a **right foot forward scissor stance** (Migi ashi hasamidachi) as you simultaneously execute a fast **right knife hand block** (Migi te shuto uke). Execute a fast **left knife hand block** (Hidari te shuto uke). Leaving the left hand in place, execute a second **right knife hand block** (Migi te shuto uke) slowly with tension to form a **lower backhand cross block** (Gedan haisho juji uke).
9) Moving your left foot back, step into a **right foot forward offensive straddle stance** (Migi ashi kougeki shikodachi). Simultaneously, bring your hands over your head in a circular motion, keeping them crossed. Chamber your hands to your left shoulder. Execute a **right inverted ridge hand** (Migi te haito) to the axilla. Look 180° and bring your right hand up to your head to chamber for a **knife hand**. Turn 180° into a **left foot forward scissor stance** (Hidari ashi hasamidachi) as you simultaneously execute a **right upper knife hand** (Migi te jodan shuto). Execute a **right front kick** (Migi ashi mae geri). Land forward and step into a **right foot forward scissor stance** (Migi ashi hasamidachi) as you simultaneously execute a fast **right knife hand block** (Migi te shuto uke). Execute a fast **left knife hand block** (Hidari te shuto uke). Leaving the left hand in

place, execute a second **right knife hand block** (Migi te shuto uke) slowly with tension to form a **lower backhand cross block** (Gedan haisho juji uke).

10) Moving your left foot back, step into a **right foot forward offensive straddle stance** (Migi ashi kougeki shikodachi). Simultaneously, bring your hands over your head in a circular motion, keeping them crossed. Chamber your hands to your left shoulder. Execute a **right inverted ridge hand** (Migi te haito) to the axilla. Look 180° and bring your right hand up to your head to chamber for a **knife hand**. Turn 180° into a **left foot forward scissor stance** (Hidari ashi hasamidachi) as you simultaneously execute a **right upper knife hand** (Migi te jodan shuto).

11) Step up into an **attention stance** (Musubidachi) and bring your right hand into an **upper backhand block** (Migi te jodan haisho uke) in front of your face. Slowly rotate your arm out to your right and execute a **right upper back hand block** (Migi te jodan haisho uke).

Finish by remaining in an **attention stance** (Musubidachi) and bringing the hand together as if for **yoi**.
Bring the hands down to groin level as usual for **yoi**, then bow.

# Rho Hai Sho

# Vision of a Crane Minor

Start from the **ready stance** (Uchihachiji dachi – at position A).

1) Pull your fists to your hips (Tsuki).

2) Step forward with your right foot into a **kneeling sword stance** (Iai dachi), executing a **lower cross hand block** (Gedan juji uke). **Kiai**.

3) Step up and through with the right leg on a 45° angle into a **right foot forward offensive straddle stance** (Migi ashi kougeki shikodachi). Perform a **double upper forearm block**.

Execute a **double shoulder punch** (Morote kata zuki), facing towards the right.

4) Extend the left hand forward to grab.

Step forward with your right foot into a **right foot forward offensive straddle stance** (Migi ashi kougeki shikodachi) and strike your outstretched hand with a **right elbow strike** (Migi te embi).

Step back with the right foot into a **left foot forward scissor stance** (Hidari ashi hasamidachi) and chamber for a **right down block** (Migi te gedan uke).

Execute a **heaven and earth posture** (Zenshi-no-kamae).

5) Step forward with left foot into a **left foot forward offensive straddle stance** (Hidari ashi kougeki shikodachi) and chamber for a **left down block** (Hidari te gedan uke).

Step back with the left foot into a **right foot forward scissor stance** (Migi ashi hasamidachi) and execute a **heaven and earth posture (Zenshi-no-kamae).**

Push the left foot back into a **right foot forward front stance** (Migi ashi zenkutsudachi) and chamber for a **right down block** (Migi te gedan uke).

Execute a **right down block** (Migi te gedan uke).

**Reverse view**

**Reverse view**

Bring the left foot in to meet the right foot and push back towards the front into a **left foot forward front stance** (Hidari ashi zenkutsudachi) while swinging the right hand up and around.

Execute a **left center punch** (Hidari te chuudan jun zuki).

6) Step forward with the right foot into a **right foot forward front stance** (Migi ashi zenkutsudachi) and execute a **right chasing punch** (Migi te oizuki).

Step forward into a **left foot forward front stance** (Hidari ashi zenkutsudachi).

Twist into a **left foot forward defensive straddle stance** (Hidari ashi boubi shikodachi) and execute a **left shoulder punch** (Hidari te kata zuki). **Kiai.**

Draw the left foot back into a **left foot forward cat stance** (Hidari ashi neko ashidachi) and execute a **right upper knife hand block** (Migi te jodan shuto uke) and a **left lower palm heel block** (Hidari te gedan shotei uke).

7) Turn into a **left foot forward scissor stance** (Hidari ashi hasamidachi) as you simultaneously execute a **right upper knife hand** (Migi te jodan shuto). Keep the left hand, at tsuki, open.

Execute a **right front kick** (Migi ashi mae geri).

Land forward and step into a **right foot forward scissor stance** (Migi ashi hasamidachi) as you simultaneously execute a fast **right knife hand block** (Migi te shuto uke).

Execute a fast **left knife hand block** (Hidari te shuto uke).

Leaving the left hand in place, execute a second **right knife hand block** (Migi te shuto uke) slowly with tension to form a **lower backhand cross block** (Gedan haisho juji uke).

8) Step back with the left foot into a **right foot forward offensive straddle stance** (Migi ashi kougeki shikodachi) and pull both hands to the right axilla with the backs of the hands touching.

Execute a **right shoulder punch** (Migi te kata zuki).

Swing the right around across to face the rear (position A).

Execute a **left shoulder punch** (Hidari te kata zuki).

Step through with the right leg towards the rear of the room into a **right foot forward offensive straddle stance** (Migi ashi kougeki shikodachi) and execute a **right shoulder punch** (Migi te kata zuki).

Bring the left foot in to meet the right and push it towards the front of the room to end in a **left foot forward front stance** (Hidari ashi zenkutsudachi) and swing the right arm across to face front.

Execute a **left center punch** (Hidari te chuudan jun zuki).

9) Execute a **right center reverse punch** (Migi te chuudan gyaku zuki).

Execute a **left center punch** (Hidari te chuudan jun zuki). **Kiai**.

Yame) Bring the right foot together with the left to an **attention stance** (Musubidachi) and finish.

Students <u>testing for 1<sup>st</sup> kyu brown belt must</u>
<u>know the form Rho Hai Sho.</u>

**Rho Hai Sho: Vision of a Crane Minor**

**Counts:**

1) Pull your fists to your hips (Tsuki).
2) Step forward with your right foot into a **kneeling sword stance** (Iai dachi), executing a lower cross hand block (Gedan juji uke). **Kiai**.
3) Step up and through with the right leg on a 45° angle into a **right foot forward offensive straddle stance** (Migi ashi kougeki shikodachi). Perform a **double upper forearm block**. Execute a **double shoulder punch** (Morote kata zuki), facing towards the right.
4) Extend the left hand forward to grab. Step forward with your right foot into a **right foot forward offensive straddle stance** (Migi ashi kougeki shikodachi) and strike your outstretched hand with a **right elbow strike** (Migi te embi). Step back with the right foot into a **left foot forward scissor stance** (Hidari ashi hasamidachi) and execute a **heaven and earth posture** (Zenshi-no-kamae).
5) Step forward with left foot into a **left foot forward offensive straddle stance** (Hidari ashi kougeki shikodachi) and stack the arms. Step back with the right foot into **left foot forward scissor stance** (Hidari ashi hasamidachi) and execute a **heaven and earth posture** (Zenshi-no-kamae). Push the left foot back into a **right foot forward front stance** (Migi ashi zenkutsudachi) and chamber for a **right down block** (Migi te gedan uke). Execute a **right down block** (Migi te gedan uke). Bring the left foot in to meet the right foot and push back towards the front of the room into a **left foot forward front stance** (Hidari ashi zenkutsudachi) while swinging the right hand up and around. Execute a **left center punch** (Hidari te chuudan jun zuki).
6) Step forward with the right foot into a **transitional stance** and execute a **right chasing punch** (Migi te oizuki). Step forward with the left leg into **a left foot forward defensive straddle stance** (Hidari ashi boubi shikodachi) and execute a **left shoulder punch** (Hidari te kata zuki). **Kiai**. Draw the left foot back into a **left foot forward cat stance** (Hidari ashi neko ashidachi) and execute a **right upper knife hand block** (Migi te jodan shuto uke) and a **left lower palm heel block** (Hidari te gedan shotei uke).
7) Turn into a **left foot forward scissor stance** (Hidari ashi hasamidachi) as you simultaneously execute a **right upper knife hand** (Migi te jodan shuto). Keep the left hand, at tsuki, open. Execute a **right front kick** (Migi ashi mae geri). Land forward and step into a **right foot forward scissor stance** (Migi ashi hasamidachi) as you simultaneously execute a fast **right knife hand block** (Migi te shuto uke). Execute a fast **left knife hand block** (Hidari te shuto uke). Leaving the left hand in place, execute a second **right knife hand block** (Migi te shuto uke) slowly with tension to form a **lower backhand cross block** (Gedan haisho juji uke).

8) Step back with the left foot into a **right foot forward offensive straddle stance** (Migi ashi kougeki shikodachi) and pull both hands to the right axilla with the backs of the hands touching.  Execute a **right shoulder punch** (Migi te kata zuki).  Swing the right around across to face the rear of the room.  Execute a **left shoulder punch** (Hidari te kata zuki).  Step through with the right leg towards the rear of the room into a **right foot forward offensive straddle stance** (Migi ashi kougeki shikodachi) and execute a **right shoulder punch** (Migi te kata zuki).  Bring the left foot in to meet the right and push it towards the front of the room to end in a **left foot forward front stance** (Hidari ashi zenkutsudachi) and swing the right arm across to face front.  Execute a **left center punch** (Hidari te chuudan jun zuki).

9) Execute a **right center reverse punch** (Migi te chuudan gyaku zuki).  Execute a **left center punch** (Hidari te chuudan jun zuki).  **Kiai**.

# Kihon Kata - Nunchaku

# Basic Nunchaku Form

Start from the **ready stance** (Uchihachiji dachi – at position A).

1) Raise right hand back with nigiri pointing upwards at a slight angle away from your back.

Strike across the upper body from right to left, allow the weapon to swing around to your back.

Strike across the upper body from left to right.

Rotating your shoulder, execute an upward strike to the chin.

Catch the weapon with your left hand behind the right shoulder.

2) With the left hand, strike upward to the chin, allowing the weapon to come over your left shoulder.

Strike across the upper body from left to right, allow the weapon to swing around to your back.

Strike across the body from right to left.

Rotating your shoulder, execute an upward strike to the chin.

Catch the weapon with your right hand behind your left shoulder.

3) With the right hand, strike upward to the chin.

Allow the weapon to come over your right shoulder.

Strike across the upper body from right to left, allow the weapon to swing around to your back.

Strike across the upper body from left to right.

Rotating your shoulder, execute an upward strike to the chin and catch the weapon with your left hand behind the right shoulder.

4) Execute an **upper block** (Jodan uke).

With the left hand, strike across the upper body from left to right, allow the weapon to swing around to your back.

Strike across the body from right to left.

Rotating your shoulder, execute an upward strike to the chin.

Catch the weapon with your right hand behind your left shoulder.

5) Execute an **upper block** (Jodan uke).

With the right hand, strike across the upper body from right to left, allow the weapon to swing around to your back.

Strike across the upper body from left to right.

Rotating your shoulder, execute an upward strike to the chin.

Catch the weapon with your left hand behind the right shoulder.

6) Execute an **upper block** (Jodan uke).

Kihon Kata - Nunchaku

With the right hand, strike across the upper body from right to left, allow the weapon to swing around to your back.

Strike across the upper body from left to right.

Rotating your shoulder, execute an upward strike to the chin.

Allow the weapon to contact your back/shoulder.

Reverse direction and strike straight forward towards an opponent in front of you, allowing the weapon to contact your inner thigh. **Kiai**.

Reverse direction, striking straight up towards an opponent in front of you.

Allow the weapon to contact your back/shoulder.

Strike across the upper body from right to left, allow the weapon to swing around to your back.

Strike across the upper body from left to right.

Rotating your shoulder, execute an upward strike to the chin.

Catch the weapon with your left hand behind the right shoulder.

7) Execute an **upper block** (Jodan uke).

With the left hand, strike across the upper body from left to right, allow the weapon to swing around to your back.

Strike across the body from right to left.

Rotating your shoulder, execute an upward strike to the chin.

Allow the weapon to contact your back/shoulder.

Reverse direction and strike straight forward towards an opponent in front of you, allowing the weapon to contact your inner thigh. **Kiai**.

Reverse direction, striking straight up towards an opponent in front of you.

Kihon Kata - Nunchaku

Allow the weapon to contact your back/shoulder.

Strike across the upper body from left to right, allow the weapon to swing around to your back.

Strike across the body from right to left.

Rotating your shoulder, execute an upward strike to the chin.

Catch the weapon with your right hand behind your left shoulder.

8) Return to yoi position.

Finish by bringing the left foot to meet the right in **attention stance** (Musubidachi) and bring the nigiri together without clacking.

Slide the right hand towards atama and flip the weapon over so atama is pointing towards you.

Lower the weapon to your left side and bow.

Kihon Kata - Nunchaku

Students testing for 5<sup>th</sup> kyu blue belt must
know the form Kihon Kata - Nunchaku.

**Kihon Kata - Nunchaku: Basic Nunchaku Form**

**Counts:**
1) Raise right hand back with nigiri pointing upwards at a slight angle away from your back. Strike across the upper body from right to left, allow the weapon to swing around to your back. Strike across the upper body from left to right. Rotating your shoulder, execute an upward strike to the chin. Catch the weapon with your left hand behind the right shoulder.
2) With the left hand, strike upward to the chin, allowing the weapon to come over your left shoulder. Strike across the upper body from left to right, allow the weapon to swing around to your back. Strike across the body from right to left. Rotating your shoulder, execute an upward strike to the chin. Catch the weapon with your right hand behind your left shoulder.
3) With the right hand, strike upward to the chin. Allow the weapon to come over your right shoulder. Strike across the upper body from right to left, allow the weapon to swing around to your back. Strike across the upper body from left to right. Rotating your shoulder, execute an upward strike to the chin and catch the weapon with your left hand behind the right shoulder.
4) Execute an **upper block** (Jodan uke). With the left hand, strike across the upper body from left to right, allow the weapon to swing around to your back. Strike across the body from right to left. Rotating your shoulder, execute an upward strike to the chin. Catch the weapon with your right hand behind your left shoulder.
5) Execute an **upper block** (Jodan uke). With the right hand, strike across the upper body from right to left, allow the weapon to swing around to your back. Strike across the upper body from left to right. Rotating your shoulder, execute an upward strike to the chin. Catch the weapon with your left hand behind the right shoulder.
6) Execute an **upper block** (Jodan uke). With the right hand, strike across the upper body from right to left, allow the weapon to swing around to your back. Strike across the upper body from left to right. Rotating your shoulder, execute an upward strike to the chin. Allow the weapon to contact your back/shoulder. Reverse direction and strike straight forward towards an opponent in front of you, allowing the weapon to contact your inner thigh. **Kiai**. Reverse direction, striking straight up towards an opponent in front of you. Allow the weapon to contact your back/shoulder. Strike across the upper body from right to left, allow the weapon to swing around to your back. Strike across the upper body from left to right. Rotating your shoulder, execute an upward strike to the chin. Catch the weapon with your left hand behind the right shoulder.
7) Execute an **upper block** (Jodan uke). With the left hand, strike across the upper body from left to right, allow the weapon to swing around to your back. Strike across the body from right to left. Rotating your shoulder, execute an upward strike to the chin. Allow the weapon to contact your back/shoulder. Reverse direction and strike straight forward towards an opponent in front of you, allowing the weapon to contact your inner thigh. **Kiai**. Reverse direction, striking straight up towards an opponent in front of you. Allow the weapon to contact your back/shoulder. Strike across the upper body from left to right, allow the weapon to swing around to your back. Strike across the body from right to left. Rotating your shoulder, execute an upward strike to the chin. Catch the weapon with your right hand behind your left shoulder.
8) Return to yoi position.

# Kihon Kata Shodan - Nunchaku

# First Basic Nunchaku Form

Start from the **ready stance** (Uchihachiji dachi – at position A).

1) Raise right hand back with nigiri pointing upwards at a slight angle away from your back.

Strike across the upper body from right to left, allow the weapon to swing around to your back.

Strike across the upper body from left to right.

Rotating your shoulder, execute an upward strike to the chin.

Catch the weapon with your left hand behind the right shoulder.

2) With the left hand, strike upward to the chin, allowing the weapon to come over your left shoulder.

Strike across the upper body from left to right, allow the weapon to swing around to your back.

Strike across the body from right to left.

Rotating your shoulder, execute an upward strike to the chin.

Catch the weapon with your right hand behind your left shoulder.

3) With the right hand, strike upward to the chin.

Allow the weapon to come over your right shoulder.

Strike across the upper body from right to left, allow the weapon to swing around to your back.

Strike across the upper body from left to right.

Rotating your shoulder, execute an upward strike to the chin and catch the weapon with your left hand behind the right shoulder.

4) Execute an **upper block** (Jodan uke).

With the left hand, strike across the upper body from left to right, allow the weapon to swing around to your back.

Strike across the body from right to left.

Rotating your shoulder, execute an upward strike to the chin.

Catch the weapon with your right hand behind your left shoulder.

5) Execute an **upper block** (Jodan uke).

With the right hand, strike across the upper body from right to left, allow the weapon to swing around to your back.

Strike across the upper body from left to right.

Rotating your shoulder, execute an upward strike to the chin.

Catch the weapon with your left hand behind the right shoulder.

6) Step forward into a **left foot forward front stance** (Hidari ashi zenkutsudachi) and with the left hand, strike upward to the chin.

Allow the weapon to come over your left shoulder.

Strike across the upper body from left to right, allow the weapon to swing around to your back..

Strike across the body from right to left.

Rotating your shoulder, execute an upward strike to the chin.

Catch the weapon with your right hand behind your left shoulder.

7) Step forward into a **right foot forward front stance** (Migi ashi zenkutsudachi) and with the right hand, strike upward to the chin.

Allow the weapon to contact your back/shoulder.

Strike across the upper body from right to left, allow the weapon to swing around to your back.

Strike across the upper body from left to right.

Rotating your shoulder, execute an upward strike to the chin.

Catch the weapon with your left hand behind the right shoulder.

8) Step backward into a **left foot forward front stance** (Hidari ashi zenkutsudachi) and with the left hand, strike upward to the chin.

Allow the weapon to contact your back/shoulder.

Strike across the upper body from left to right, allow the weapon to swing around to your back..

Strike across the body from right to left.

Rotating your shoulder, execute an upward strike to the chin.

Catch the weapon with your right hand behind your left shoulder.

9) Step back into a **right foot forward front stance** (Migi ashi zenkutsudachi) and with the right hand, strike upward to the chin.

Kihon Kata Shodan - Nunchaku

Allow the weapon to contact your back/shoulder.

Strike across the upper body from right to left, allow the weapon to swing around to your back.

Strike across the body from left to right.

Rotating your shoulder, execute an upward strike to the chin.

Catch the weapon with your left hand behind the right shoulder.

Bring the left leg up to meet the right leg and chamber the weapon behind you on the right side, keeping the nigiri each at an angle to eachother.

Step out with the left foot into a **left foot forward defensive straddle stance** (Hidari ashi boubi shikodachi) and bring the weapon across your chest in front of you, with the nigiri at slight angles for a **middle section guarding block**.

**Side view**

10) Shift into a **left foot forward front stance** (Hidari ashi zenkutsudachi) and execute an upper block (Jodan uke).

With the right hand, strike across the upper body from right to left, allow the weapon to swing around to your back. **Kiai**.

Strike across the upper body from left to right.

Rotating your shoulder, execute an upward strike to the chin.

Catch the weapon with your left hand behind the right shoulder.

With the left hand, strike upward to the chin, allowing the weapon to come over your left shoulder.

Strike across the upper body from left to right, allow the weapon to swing around to your back.

Strike across the body from right to left.

Rotating your shoulder, execute an upward strike to the chin.

Catch the weapon with your right hand behind your left shoulder.

Bring the right foot up to meet the left foot and chamber the weapon behind you on the left side, keeping the nigiri each at an angle to eachother.

Step out with the left foot into a **right foot forward defensive straddle stance** (Migi ashi boubi shikodachi) and bring the weapon across your chest in front of you, with the nigiri at slight angles for a **middle section guarding block**.

11) Shift into a **right foot forward front stance** (Migi ashi zenkutsudachi) and execute an upper block (Jodan uke).

With the left hand, strike across the upper body from left to right, allow the weapon to swing around to your back. **Kiai**.

Strike across the body from right to left.

Rotating your shoulder, execute an upward strike to the chin.

Catch the weapon with your right hand behind your left shoulder.

With the right hand, strike upward to the chin, allowing the weapon to come over your right shoulder.

Strike across the upper body from right to left, allow the weapon to swing around to your back.

Strike across the upper body from left to right.

Rotating your shoulder, execute an upward strike to the chin.

Catch the weapon with your left hand behind the right shoulder.

Bring the left foot in to meet the right and push it out into a **ready stance** (Uchihachiji dachi) facing front, pushing the weapon to yoi position.

12) Raise right hand back with nigiri pointing upwards at a slight angle away from your back.

Strike across the upper body from right to left, allow the weapon to swing around to your back.

Strike across the upper body from left to right.

Rotating your shoulder, execute an upward strike to the chin.

Allow the weapon to contact your back/shoulder.

Reverse direction and strike straight forward towards an opponent in front of you, allowing the weapon to contact your inner thigh.

Reverse direction, striking straight up towards an opponent in front of you.

Allow the weapon to contact your back/shoulder.

Strike across the upper body from right to left, allow the weapon to swing around to your back.

Strike across the upper body from left to right.

Rotating your shoulder, execute an upward strike to the chin.

Catch the weapon with your left hand behind the right shoulder.

13) Execute an **upper block** (Jodan uke).

With the left hand, strike across the upper body from left to right, allow the weapon to swing around to your back.

Strike across the body from right to left.

Rotating your shoulder, execute an upward strike to the chin.

Allow the weapon to contact your back/shoulder.

Reverse direction and strike straight forward towards an opponent in front of you, allowing the weapon to contact your inner thigh.

Reverse direction, striking straight up towards an opponent in front of you.

Allow the weapon to contact your back/shoulder.

Strike across the upper body from left to right, allow the weapon to swing around to your back.

Strike across the body from right to left.

Rotating your shoulder, execute an upward strike to the chin.

Catch the weapon with your right hand behind your left shoulder.

14) Return to yoi position.

Finish by bringing the left foot to meet the right in **attention stance** (Musubidachi) and bring the nigiri together without clacking.

Slide the right hand towards atama and flip the weapon over so atama is pointing towards you.

Lower the weapon to your left side.

Bow

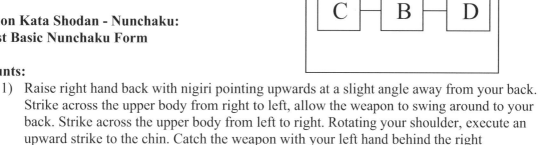

Students testing for 4<sup>th</sup> kyu green belt must
know the form Kihon Kata Shodan - Nunchaku.

**Kihon Kata Shodan - Nunchaku:**
**First Basic Nunchaku Form**

**Counts:**

1) Raise right hand back with nigiri pointing upwards at a slight angle away from your back. Strike across the upper body from right to left, allow the weapon to swing around to your back. Strike across the upper body from left to right. Rotating your shoulder, execute an upward strike to the chin. Catch the weapon with your left hand behind the right shoulder.

2) With the left hand, strike upward to the chin, allowing the weapon to come over your left shoulder. Strike across the upper body from left to right, allow the weapon to swing around to your back. Strike across the body from right to left. Rotating your shoulder, execute an upward strike to the chin. Catch the weapon with your right hand behind your left shoulder.

3) With the right hand, strike upward to the chin. Allow the weapon to come over your right shoulder. Strike across the upper body from right to left, allow the weapon to swing around to your back. Strike across the upper body from left to right. Rotating your shoulder, execute an upward strike to the chin and catch the weapon with your left hand behind the right shoulder.

4) Execute an **upper block** (Jodan uke). With the left hand, strike across the upper body from left to right, allow the weapon to swing around to your back. Strike across the body from right to left. Rotating your shoulder, execute an upward strike to the chin. Catch the weapon with your right hand behind your left shoulder.

5) Execute an **upper block** (Jodan uke). With the right hand, strike across the upper body from right to left, allow the weapon to swing around to your back. Strike across the upper body from left to right. Rotating your shoulder, execute an upward strike to the chin. Catch the weapon with your left hand behind the right shoulder.

6) Step forward into a **left foot forward front stance** (Hidari ashi zenkutsudachi) and with the left hand, strike upward to the chin. Allow the weapon to come over your left shoulder. Strike across the upper body from left to right. Strike across the body from right to left. Rotating your shoulder, execute an upward strike to the chin. Catch the weapon with your right hand behind your left shoulder.

7) Step forward into a **right foot forward front stance** (Migi ashi zenkutsudachi) and with the right hand, strike upward to the chin. Allow the weapon to contact your back/shoulder. Strike across the upper body from right to left, allow the weapon to swing around to your back. Strike across the upper body from left to right. Rotating your shoulder, execute an upward strike to the chin. Catch the weapon with your left hand behind the right shoulder.

8) Step backward into a **left foot forward front stance** (Hidari ashi zenkutsudachi) and with the left hand, strike upward to the chin. Allow the weapon to contact your back/shoulder. Strike across the upper body from left to right. Strike across the body from right to left. Rotating your shoulder, execute an upward strike to the chin. Catch the weapon with your right hand behind your left shoulder.

9) Step back into a **right foot forward front stance** (Migi ashi zenkutsudachi) and with the right hand, strike upward to the chin. Allow the weapon to contact your back/shoulder. Strike across the upper body from right to left, allow the weapon to swing around to your back. Strike across the body from left to right. Rotating your shoulder, execute an upward strike to the chin. Catch the weapon with your left hand behind the right shoulder. Bring

the left leg up to meet the right leg and chamber the weapon behind you on the right side, keeping the nigiri each at an angle to eachother. Step out with the left foot into a **left foot forward defensive straddle stance** (Hidari ashi boubi shikodachi) and bring the weapon across your chest in front of you, with the nigiri at slight angles for a **middle section guarding block**.

10) Shift into a **left foot forward front stance** (Hidari ashi zenkutsudachi) and execute an upper block (Jodan uke). With the right hand, strike across the upper body from right to left, allow the weapon to swing around to your back. **Kiai**. Strike across the upper body from left to right. Rotating your shoulder, execute an upward strike to the chin. Catch the weapon with your left hand behind the right shoulder. With the left hand, strike upward to the chin, allowing the weapon to come over your left shoulder. Strike across the upper body from left to right, allow the weapon to swing around to your back. Strike across the body from right to left. Rotating your shoulder, execute an upward strike to the chin. Catch the weapon with your right hand behind your left shoulder. Bring the right foot up to meet the left foot and chamber the weapon behind you on the left side, keeping the nigiri each at an angle to eachother. Step out with the left foot into a **right foot forward defensive straddle stance** (Migi ashi boubi shikodachi) and bring the weapon across your chest in front of you, with the nigiri at slight anglesfor a **middle section guarding block**.

11) Shift into a **right foot forward front stance** (Migi ashi zenkutsudachi) and execute an upper block (Jodan uke). With the left hand, strike across the upper body from left to right, allow the weapon to swing around to your back. **Kiai**. Strike across the body from right to left. Rotating your shoulder, execute an upward strike to the chin. Catch the weapon with your right hand behind your left shoulder. With the right hand, strike upward to the chin, allowing the weapon to come over your right shoulder. Strike across the upper body from right to left, allow the weapon to swing around to your back. Strike across the upper body from left to right. Rotating your shoulder, execute an upward strike to the chin. Catch the weapon with your left hand behind the right shoulder. Bring the left foot in to meet the right and push it out into a **ready stance** (Uchihachiji dachi) facing front, pushing the weapon to yoi position.

12) Raise right hand back with nigiri pointing upwards at a slight angle away from your back. Strike across the upper body from right to left, allow the weapon to swing around to your back. Strike across the upper body from left to right. Rotating your shoulder, execute an upward strike to the chin. Allow the weapon to contact your back/shoulder. Reverse direction and strike straight forward towards an opponent in front of you, allowing the weapon to contact your inner thigh. Reverse direction, striking straight up towards an opponent in front of you. Allow the weapon to contact your back/shoulder. Strike across the upper body from right to left, allow the weapon to swing around to your back. Strike across the upper body from left to right. Rotating your shoulder, execute an upward strike to the chin. Catch the weapon with your left hand behind the right shoulder.

13) Execute an **upper block** (Jodan uke). With the left hand, strike across the upper body from left to right, allow the weapon to swing around to your back. Strike across the body from right to left. Rotating your shoulder, execute an upward strike to the chin. Allow the weapon to contact your back/shoulder. Reverse direction and strike straight forward towards an opponent in front of you, allowing the weapon to contact your inner thigh. Reverse direction, striking straight up towards an opponent in front of you. Allow the weapon to contact your back/shoulder. Strike across the upper body from left to right, allow the weapon to swing around to your back. Strike across the body from right to left. Rotating your shoulder, execute an upward strike to the chin. Catch the weapon with your right hand behind your left shoulder.

14) Return to yoi position.

# Yoshu

# Continued Improvement

Start from the **ready stance** (Uchihachiji dachi – at position A).

1) Roll the weapon inward and execute a **rolling strike** to the bridge of the nose with atama.

Execute an **upper block** (Jodan uke).

Step forward into a **left foot forward defensive straddle stance** (Hidari ashi boubi shikodachi) and execute a **middle section guarding block**.

2) Step forward into a **right foot forward defensive straddle stance** (Migi ashi boubi shikodachi) and chamber over the right shoulder. Have the elbow pointed at 90 degrees to the front so you can look forward.

Strike down outside of your body space.

Strike across the body from right to left.

Strike across the upper body from left to right.

Rotating your shoulder, execute an upward strike to the chin.

Catch the weapon with your left hand behind the right shoulder. Have the elbow pointed at 90 degrees to the front so you can look forward.

3) Step forward into a **left foot forward defensive straddle stance** (Hidari ashi boubi shikodachi) and chamber over the left shoulder. Have the elbow pointed at 90 degrees to the front so you can look forward.

Strike down outside of your body space.

Strike across the upper body from left to right.

Strike across the body from right to left.

Rotating your shoulder, execute an upward strike to the chin. Catch the weapon with your right hand behind the left shoulder. Have the elbow pointed at 90 degrees to the front so you can look forward.

Bring your right foot to meet the left, then step out into a **right foot forward defensive straddle stance** (Migi ashi boubi shikodachi) and execute a **middle-section guarding block** facing position D.

4) Shift into a **right foot forward front stance** (Migi ashi zenkutsudachi) and execute an **outward upper angle block** to the right side.

**Side view**

Yoshu

Chamber the weapon over your right shoulder.

Strike down outside of your body space.

Turn your body towards the front and shift into a **left foot forward front stance** (Hidari ashi zenkutsudachi) and execute a strike from right to left, allowing the weapon to swing around to your back.

Strike across the upper body from left to right.

Perform a cross catch with your left hand.

Bring the left foot back to meet the right foot and chamber behind you.

Step into a **left foot forward defensive straddle stance** (Hidari ashi boubi shikodachi) and execute a **middle-section guarding block** facing position C.

5) Shift into a **left foot forward front stance** (Hidari ashi zenkutsudachi) and execute an **outward upper angle block** to the left side.

Chamber the weapon over your left shoulder.

Strike down outside of your body space.

Turn your body towards the front and shift into a **right foot forward front stance** (Migi ashi zenkutsudachi) and execute a strike from left to right, allowing the weapon to swing around to your back.

Strike across the body from right to left and perform a cross catch with your right hand.

Bring the right foot back to meet the left foot and chamber behind you. Step into a **right foot forward defensive straddle stance** (Migi ashi boubi shikodachi) and execute a **middle-section guarding block** facing front.

6) Shift into a **right foot forward front stance** (Migi ashi zenkutsudachi) and execute an **outward upper angle block** to the right side.

Chamber the weapon over your right shoulder.

Strike down outside of your body space.

Turn your body towards position C and shift into a **left foot forward front stance** (Hidari ashi zenkutsudachi) and execute a strike from right to left, allowing the weapon to swing around to your back.

Turn your body towards the front and shift into a **right foot forward front stance** (Migi ashi zenkutsudachi) and execute a strike from left to right.

Rotating your shoulder, execute an upward strike to the chin.

Catch the weapon with your left hand behind your back.

Holding on with the left hand, bring the weapon around the body from left to right.

Continue the momentum arcing over your head.

Continue the momentum arcing over your head.

Strike across the body from left to right, allow the weapon to swing around to your back.

Strike across the body from right to left.

Perform a cross catch with your right hand.

7) Transition to a **left one-legged stance** (Hidari ashi ippon ashidachi) and chamber the weapon over the right shoulder.

Strike down outside of your body space.

Set the right foot down into a **left facing shoulder stance** (Hidari ashi zenkutsudachi at an angle) and strike right to left, allow the weapon to swing around to your back. **Kiai.**

Strike across the body from left to right.

Performed a cross catch with the left hand.

Transition to a **right one-legged stance** (Migi ashi ippon ashidachi) and chamber the weapon over the left shoulder.

Strike down outside of your body space then step back into a **right foot forward front stance** (Migi ashi zenkutsudachi).

Strike across the upper body from left to right, allow the weapon to swing around to your back.

Strike across the body from right to left.

Rotating your shoulder, execute an upward strike to the chin.

Yoshu

Catch the weapon with your right hand behind your left shoulder.

With the right hand, strike upward to the chin.

Allow the weapon to contact your back/shoulder.

Strike across the upper body from right to left, allow the weapon to swing around to your back.

Strike across the upper body from left to right.

Rotating your shoulder, execute an upward strike to the chin.

Continue the strike through another spin.

Continue the strike through the second spin to strike the chin.

Catch the weapon with your left hand behind the right shoulder.

8) Step forward into a **left foot forward front stance** (Hidari ashi zenkutsudachi) and with the left hand, strike upward to the chin, allow the weapon to contact your back/shoulder.

Strike across the upper body from left to right, allow the weapon to swing around to your back.

Strike across the body from right to left.

Rotating your shoulder, execute an upward strike to the chin. Continue the strike through another spin. Continue the strike through the second spin to strike the chin.

Catch the weapon with your right hand behind your left shoulder.

9) Release the weapon with the left hand and bring the weapon up toward your right shoulder with the right hand as you begin to jump.

Allow the weapon to contact your back/shoulder.

Jump with the right foot landing where the left foot was and step out with the left foot.

Land in a **left foot forward front stance** (Hidari ashi zenkutsudachi) as you strike from right to left, allow the weapon to swing around to your back. **Kiai**.

124

Strike across the body from left to right.

Perform a cross catch with the left hand.

Bring the right foot back to meet the left foot and chamber behind you. Step into a **right foot forward defensive straddle stance** (Migi ashi boubi shikodachi) and execute a **middle-section guarding block** facing rear.

**Reverse view**

10) Shift into a **right foot forward front stance** (Migi ashi zenkutsudachi) and execute a right hand clearing strike.

Bring the weapon back from right to left and catch with the left hand in an upward position.

After catching, allow the weapon to come over your left forearm as you begin to strike to the right.

Strike across the upper body from left to right, allow the weapon to swing around to your back.

Strike across the body from right to left.

Rotating your shoulder, execute an upward strike to the chin.

Catch the weapon with your right hand behind your left shoulder.

With the right hand, strike upward to the chin, allowing the weapon to come over your left shoulder.

Strike across the upper body from right to left, allow the weapon to swing around to your back.

Strike across the upper body from left to right.

Rotating your shoulder, execute an upward strike to the chin.

Catch the weapon with your left hand behind the right shoulder.

11) Step forward into a **left foot forward front stance** (Hidari ashi zenkutsudachi) and with the left hand, strike upward to the chin.

Allow the weapon to contact your back/shoulder.

Strike across the upper body from left to right, allow the weapon to swing around to your back.

Strike across the body from right to left.

Rotating your shoulder, execute an upward strike to the chin.

Catch the weapon with your right hand behind your left shoulder.

12) Release the weapon with the left hand and bring the weapon up toward your right shoulder with the right hand as you begin to jump.

Continue your strike through the jump.

Allow the weapon to contact your back/shoulder. Jump with the right foot landing where the left foot was and step out with the left foot.

Land in a **ready stance** (Uchihachijidachi) as you strike from right to left, twisting your hips, and allow the weapon to swing around to your back. **Kiai.**

Strike across the body from left to right and transition to yoi stance (Uchihachijidachi).

Rotating your shoulder, execute an upward strike to the chin.

Allow the weapon to contact your back/shoulder.

Reverse direction and strike straight forward towards an opponent in front of you, allowing the weapon to contact your inner thigh.

Reverse direction, striking straight up towards an opponent in front of you, allow the weapon to contact your back/shoulder.

Strike across the upper body from right to left, allow the weapon to swing around to your back.

Strike across the upper body from left to right.

Rotating your shoulder, execute an upward strike to the chin. Continue the strike through another spin. Continue the strike through the second spin to strike the chin.

Bring the weapon over your right shoulder as if to catch, but only allow it to touch your left hand before reversing direction.

Spin the shiri counter clockwise.

Continue the strike through another spin.

Catch the weapon in your right axilla.

Reverse direction, striking upward to the chin with the right hand, allow the weapon to come over your right shoulder.

Strike across the upper body from right to left, allow the weapon to swing around to your back.

Strike across the upper body from left to right.

Rotating your shoulder, execute an upward strike to the chin.

Catch the weapon with your left hand behind the right shoulder.

13) With the left hand, strike upward to the chin, allow the weapon to contact your back/shoulder.

Strike across the upper body from left to right, allow the weapon to swing around to your back..

Strike across the body from right to left.

Rotating your shoulder, execute an upward strike to the chin, allow the weapon to contact your back/shoulder.

Reverse direction and strike straight forward towards an opponent in front of you, allowing the weapon to contact your inner thigh.

Reverse direction, striking straight up towards an opponent in front of you, allow the weapon to contact your back/shoulder.

Strike across the upper body from left to right, allow the weapon to swing around to your back.

Strike across the body from right to left.

Rotating your shoulder, execute an upward strike to the chin. Continue the strike through another spin. Continue the strike through the second spin to strike the chin.

Bring the weapon over your left shoulder as if to catch, but only allow it to touch your right hand before reversing direction.

Spin the shiri counter clockwise. Continue the strike through another spin.

Yoshu

130

Catch the weapon in your left axilla.

Reverse direction, striking upward to the chin with the left hand, allow the weapon to come over your left shoulder.

Strike across the upper body from left to right, allow the weapon to swing around to your back.

Strike across the body from right to left.

Rotating your shoulder, execute an upward strike to the chin.

Catch the weapon with your right hand behind your left shoulder.

Step forward into a **left foot forward defensive straddle stance** (Hidari ashi boubi shikodachi) and execute a **middle-section guarding block**.

14) Shift into a **left foot forward front stance** (Hidari ashi zenkutsudachi) and execute an **upper block** (Jodan uke).

Strike across the upper body from right to left, allow the weapon to swing around to your back. **Kiai.**

Rotating your shoulder, execute an upward strike to the chin.

Continue the strike through another spin.

Continue the strike through the second spin to strike the chin.

Bring the weapon over your right shoulder as if to catch, but only allow it to touch your left hand before reversing direction.

Spin the shiri counter clockwise.

Continue the strike through another spin.

Continue the strike through the second spin.

Catch the weapon in your right axilla.

Strike down outside of your body space.

Yoshu

132

Begin a figure eight patten by directing the shiri clockwise to the left across your body.

Continue the figure 8 pattern by directing the shiri clockwise to the left across your body.

Continue the figure eight patten by directing the shiri clockwise to the right across your body.

Finish the figure 8 pattern by directing the shiri clockwise to the left across your body and again to the right across your body then continue to an upward strike to the chin.

Catch the weapon with your left hand behind the right shoulder.

15) Step up to **attention stance** (Musubidachi).

With the left hand, strike upward to the chin, allow the weapon to come over your left shoulder. **Kiai**.

Strike across the upper body from left to right, allow the weapon to swing around to your back.

Strike across the body from right to left.

Yoshu

Rotating your shoulder, execute an upward strike to the chin.

Catch the weapon with your right hand behind your left shoulder.

16) Return to yoi position.

Bring the nigiri together without clacking.

Slide the right hand towards atama and flip the weapon over so atama is pointing towards you.

Lower the weapon to your left side.

Bow.

Students testing for Shodan must
know the form Yoshu.

**Yoshu: Continued Improvement**

**Counts:**
1) Roll the weapon inward and execute a **rolling strike** to the bridge of the nose with atama. Execute an **upper block** (Jodan uke). Step forward into a **left foot forward defensive straddle stance** (Hidari ashi boubi shikodachi) and execute a **middle-section guarding block**.
2) Step forward into a **right foot forward defensive straddle stance** (Migi ashi boubi shikodachi) and chamber over the right shoulder. Have the elbow pointed at 90 degrees to the front so you can look forward. Strike down outside of your body space. Strike across the body from right to left. Strike across the upper body from left to right. Rotating your shoulder, execute an upward strike to the chin. Catch the weapon with your left hand behind the right shoulder. Have the elbow pointed at 90 degrees to the front so you can look forward.
3) Step forward into a **left foot forward defensive straddle stance** (Hidari ashi boubi shikodachi) and chamber over the left shoulder. Have the elbow pointed at 90 degrees to the front so you can look forward. Strike down outside of your body space. Strike across the upper body from left to right. Strike across the body from right to left. Rotating your shoulder, execute an upward strike to the chin. Catch the weapon with your right hand behind the left shoulder. Have the elbow pointed at 90 degrees to the front so you can look forward. Bring your right foot to meet the left, then step out into a **right foot forward defensive straddle stance** (Migi ashi boubi shikodachi) and execute a **middle-section guarding block** facing position D.
4) Shift into a **right foot forward front stance** (Migi ashi zenkutsudachi) and execute an **outward upper angle block** to the right side. Chamber the weapon over your right shoulder. Strike down outside of your body space. Turn your body towards the front and shift into a **left foot forward front stance** (Hidari ashi zenkutsudachi) and execute a strike from right to left, allowing the weapon to swing around to your back. Strike across the upper body from left to right. Perform a cross catch with your left hand. Bring the left foot back to meet the right foot and chamber behind you. Step into a **left foot forward defensive straddle stance** (Hidari ashi boubi shikodachi) and execute a **middle-section guarding block** facing position C.
5) Shift into a **left foot forward front stance** (Hidari ashi zenkutsudachi) and execute an **outward upper angle block** to the left side. Chamber the weapon over your left shoulder. Strike down outside of your body space. Turn your body towards the front and shift into a **right foot forward front stance** (Migi ashi zenkutsudachi) and execute a strike from left to right, allowing the weapon to swing around to your back. Strike across the body from right to left and perform a cross catch with your right hand. Bring the right foot back to meet the left foot and chamber behind you. Step into a **right foot forward defensive straddle stance** (Migi ashi boubi shikodachi) and execute a **middle-section guarding block** facing front.
6) Shift into a **right foot forward front stance** (Migi ashi zenkutsudachi) and execute an **outward upper angle block** to the right side. Chamber the weapon over your right shoulder. Strike down outside of your body space. Turn your body towards position C and shift into a **left foot forward front stance** (Hidari ashi zenkutsudachi) and execute a

strike from right to left, allowing the weapon to swing around to your back. Turn your body towards the front and shift into a **right foot forward front stance** (Migi ashi zenkutsudachi) and execute a strike from left to right. Rotating your shoulder, execute an upward strike to the chin. Catch the weapon with your left hand behind your back. Holding on with the left hand, bring the weapon around the body from left to right. Continue the momentum arcing over your head. Strike across the body from left to right, allow the weapon to swing around to your back. Strike across the body from right to left. Perform a cross catch with your right hand.

7) Transition to a **left one-legged stance** (Hidari ashi ippon ashidachi) and chamber the weapon over the right shoulder. Strike down outside of your body space. Set the right foot down into a **left leg shoulder stance** (Hidari ashi zenkutsudachi at an angle) and strike right to left, allow the weapon to swing around to your back. **Kiai.** Strike across the body from left to right. Performed a cross catch with the left hand. Transition to a **right one-legged stance** (Migi ashi ippon ashidachi) and chamber the weapon over the left shoulder. Strike down outside of your body space then step back into a **right foot forward front stance** (Migi ashi zenkutsudachi). Strike across the upper body from left to right, allow the weapon to swing around to your back. Strike across the body from right to left. Rotating your shoulder, execute an upward strike to the chin. Catch the weapon with your right hand behind your left shoulder. With the right hand, strike upward to the chin. Allow the weapon to contact your back/shoulder. Strike across the upper body from right to left, allow the weapon to swing around to your back. Strike across the upper body from left to right. Rotating your shoulder, execute an upward strike to the chin. Continue the strike through another spin. Continue the strike through the second spin to strike the chin. Catch the weapon with your left hand behind the right shoulder.

8) Step forward into a **left foot forward front stance** (Hidari ashi zenkutsudachi) and with the left hand, strike upward to the chin, allow the weapon to contact your back/shoulder. Strike across the upper body from left to right, allow the weapon to swing around to your back. Strike across the body from right to left. Rotating your shoulder, execute an upward strike to the chin. Continue the strike through another spin. Continue the strike through the second spin to strike the chin. Catch the weapon with your right hand behind your left shoulder.

9) Release the weapon with the left hand and execute an upward strike to the chin with the right hand as you begin to jump. Allow the weapon to contact your back/shoulder. Jump with the right foot landing where the left foot was and step out with the left foot. Land in a **left foot forward front stance** (Hidari ashi zenkutsudachi) as you strike from right to left, allow the weapon to swing around to your back. **Kiai.** Strike across the body from left to right. Perform a cross catch with the left hand. Bring the right foot back to meet the left foot and chamber behind you. Step into a **right foot forward defensive straddle stance** (Migi ashi boubi shikodachi) and execute a **middle-section guarding block** facing rear.

10) Shift into a **right foot forward front stance** (Migi ashi zenkutsudachi) and execute a right hand clearing strike. Bring the weapon back from right to left and catch with the left hand in an upward position. After catching, allow the weapon to come over your left forearm as you begin to strike to the right. Strike across the upper body from left to right, allow the weapon to swing around to your back. Strike across the body from right to left. Rotating your shoulder, execute an upward strike to the chin. Catch the weapon with your right hand behind your left shoulder. With the right hand, strike upward to the chin, allowing the weapon to come over your left shoulder. Strike across the upper body from right to left, allow the weapon to swing around to your back. Strike across the upper body from left to right. Rotating your shoulder, execute an upward strike to the chin. Catch the weapon with your left hand behind the right shoulder.

11) Step forward into a **left foot forward front stance** (Hidari ashi zenkutsudachi) and with the left hand, strike upward to the chin. Allow the weapon to contact your back/shoulder. Strike across the upper body from left to right, allow the weapon to swing around to your back. Strike across the body from right to left. Rotating your shoulder, execute an upward strike to the chin. Catch the weapon with your right hand behind your left shoulder.

12) Release the weapon with the left hand and execute an upward strike to the chin with the right hand as you begin to jump. Allow the weapon to contact your back/shoulder. Jump with the right foot landing where the left foot was and step out with the left foot. Land in a **left foot forward front stance** (Hidari ashi zenkutsudachi) as you strike from right to left, allow the weapon to swing around to your back. **Kiai**. Strike across the body from left to right and transition to yoi stance (Uchihachijidachi). Rotating your shoulder, execute an upward strike to the chin. Allow the weapon to contact your back/shoulder. Reverse direction and strike straight forward towards an opponent in front of you, allowing the weapon to contact your inner thigh. Reverse direction, striking straight up towards an opponent in front of you, allow the weapon to contact your back/shoulder. Strike across the upper body from right to left, allow the weapon to swing around to your back. Strike across the upper body from left to right. Rotating your shoulder, execute an upward strike to the chin. Continue the strike through another spin. Continue the strike through the second spin to strike the chin. Bring the weapon over your right shoulder as if to catch, but only allow it to touch your left hand before reversing direction. Spin the shiri counter clockwise. Continue the strike through another spin. Catch the weapon in your right axilla. Reverse direction, striking upward to the chin with the right hand, allow the weapon to come over your right shoulder. Strike across the upper body from right to left, allow the weapon to swing around to your back. Strike across the upper body from left to right. Rotating your shoulder, execute an upward strike to the chin. Catch the weapon with your left hand behind the right shoulder.

13) With the left hand, strike upward to the chin, allow the weapon to contact your back/shoulder. Strike across the upper body from left to right, allow the weapon to swing around to your back.. Strike across the body from right to left. Rotating your shoulder, execute an upward strike to the chin, allow the weapon to contact your back/shoulder. Reverse direction and strike straight forward towards an opponent in front of you, allowing the weapon to contact your inner thigh. Reverse direction, striking straight up towards an opponent in front of you, allow the weapon to contact your back/shoulder. Strike across the upper body from left to right, allow the weapon to swing around to your back. Strike across the body from right to left. Rotating your shoulder, execute an upward strike to the chin. Continue the strike through another spin. Continue the strike through the second spin to strike the chin. Bring the weapon over your left shoulder as if to catch, but only allow it to touch your right hand before reversing direction. Spin the shiri counter clockwise. Continue the strike through another spin. Catch the weapon in your left axilla. Reverse direction, striking upward to the chin with the left hand, allow the weapon to come over your left shoulder. Strike across the upper body from left to right, allow the weapon to swing around to your back. Strike across the body from right to left. Rotating your shoulder, execute an upward strike to the chin. Catch the weapon with your right hand behind your left shoulder. Step forward into a **left foot forward defensive straddle stance** (Hidari ashi boubi shikodachi) and execute a **middle-section guarding block**.

14) Shift into a **left foot forward front stance** (Hidari ashi zenkutsudachi) and execute an **upper block** (Jodan uke). Strike across the upper body from right to left, allow the weapon to swing around to your back. **Kiai**. Rotating your shoulder, execute an upward strike to the chin. Continue the strike through another spin. Bring the weapon over your right shoulder as if to catch, but only allow it to touch your left hand before reversing direction. Spin the shiri counter clockwise. Continue the strike through another spin.

Catch the weapon in your right axilla. Strike down outside of your body space. Begin a figure eight pattern by directing the shiri clockwise to the left across your body. Continue the figure 8 pattern by directing the shiri clockwise to the left across your body. Continue the figure eight patten by directing the shiri clockwise to the right across your body. Finish the figure 8 pattern by directing the shiri clockwise to the left across your body and again to the right across your body then continue to an upward strike to the chin. Catch the weapon with your left hand behind the right shoulder.

15) Step up to **attention stance** (Musubidachi). With the left hand, strike upward to the chin, allow the weapon to come over your left shoulder. **Kiai**. Strike across the upper body from left to right, allow the weapon to swing around to your back. Strike across the body from right to left. Rotating your shoulder, execute an upward strike to the chin. Catch the weapon with your right hand behind your left shoulder.

16) Return to yoi position.

# Kihon Kata Shodan - Bo

# First Basic Bo Form

Start from the **ready stance** (Hidari ashi zenkutsudachi – at position A).

1) Move your left hand from the **lower knifehand block** (Hidari te gedan shuto uke) position over the head to grab the bo staff 1/3 the way down from the B side.

2) Step forward into a **right foot front stance** (Migi ashi zenkutsudachi) then bring the A side of the bo in the right hand in a rowing motion from back to front ending in a **upper face/clavicle strike** with the A side of the bo. The left hand should end up by your left hip.

3) Bring the B side of the bo in your left hand up while keeping your right hand A side in place. The bo should end up parallel to the ground with your left hand by your left shoulder.

Step forward into a **left foot forward front stance** (Hidari ashi zenkutsudachi) and execute a **horizontal strike** with the B end of the bo, the staff ending horizontal on the right side of the body.

4) Step forward into a **right foot forward front stance** (Migi ashi zekutsudachi) and execute a **face/clavicle strike** with the A end of the staff, bringing end A from behind your right shoulder forward.

**Side view**

Move your left foot and turn 180 degrees counter-clockwise to face the rear in a **right foot forward front stance** (Migi ashi zenkutsudachi) and perform a **mid-section block** (Chuudan uke) with end A passing down next to the right leg and the staff pressing out.

**Side view**

Kihon Kata Shodan - Bo

Perform a **face/clavicle strike** with end A by having end A pulled back past the right leg in a rowing motion. The left hand should end up by the left hip. **Kiai**.

5) Bring the B side of the bo in your left hand up while keeping your right hand A side in place. The bo should end up parallel to the ground with your left hand by your left shoulder.

Step forward into a **left foot forward front stance** (Hidari ashi zenkutsudachi) and execute a **horizontal strike** with the B end of the bo, the staff ending horizontal on the right side of the body.

6) Step forward into a **right foot forward front stance** (Migi ashi zekutsudachi) and execute a **face/clavicle strike** with the A end of the staff, bringing end A from behind your right shoulder forward.

Move your left foot and turn 180 degrees counter-clockwise to face the front in a **right foot forward front stance** (Migi ashi zenkutsudachi) and perform a **mid-section block** (Chuudan uke) with end A passing down next to the right leg and the staff pressing out.

Perform a **face/clavicle strike** with end A by having end A pulled back past the right leg in a rowing motion. The left hand should end up by the left hip. **Kiai**.

7) Bring left foot forward into **attention stance** (Musubidachi) while bringing end B up and execute a upward **chin strike**.

Execute **chin strike**.

End with the staff vertical tucked into your right side with your left hand across your chest 1/3 the way down the B end and your right hand down by your right side 1/3 the way up the A end. End A should be pointing at the ground and end B should be straight up.

On the command yame move your left hand in a circular knifehand block (Shuto uke).

Continue the motion to your side.

End with the hand down at your left side.

Bow and place end A on the ground.

Straighten up leaving the bo on the ground.

Kihon Kata Shodan - Bo

142

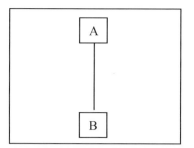

<u>Students testing for 3<sup>rd</sup> kyu green belt must
know the form Kihon Kata Shodan - Bo.</u>

**Kihon Kata Shodan - Bo: First Basic Bo Form**

**Counts:**
1) Move your left hand from the **lower knifehand block** (Hidari te gedan shuto uke) position over the head to grab the bo staff 1/3 the way down from the B side.
2) Step forward into a **right foot front stance** (Migi ashi zenkutsudachi) then bring the A side of the bo in the right hand in a rowing motion from back to front ending in a **upper face/clavicle strike** with the A side of the bo. The left hand should end up by your left hip.
3) Bring the B side of the bo in your left hand up while keeping your right hand A side in place. The bo should end up parallel to the ground with your left hand by your left shoulder. Step forward into a **left foot forward front stance** (Hidari ashi zenkutsudachi) and execute a **horizontal strike** with the B end of the bo, the staff ending horizontal on the right side of the body.
4) Step forward into a **right foot forward front stance** (Migi ashi zekutsudachi) and execute a **face/clavicle strike** with the A end of the staff, bringing end A from behind your right shoulder forward. Turning 180 degrees counter-clockwise moving only your left foot ending in a **right foot forward front stance** (Migi ashi zenktsudachi) and perform a **mid-section block** (chuudan uke) with end A passing down next to the right leg and the staff pressing out. Perform a **face/clavicle strike** with end A by having end A pulled back past the right leg in a rowing motion. The left hand should end up by the left hip. **Kiai**.
5) Bring the B side of the bo in your left hand up while keeping your right hand A side in place. The bo should end up parallel to the ground with your left hand by your left shoulder. Step forward into a **left foot forward front stance** (Hidari ashi zenkutsudachi) and execute a **horizontal strike** with the B end of the bo, the staff ending horizontal on the right side of the body.
6) Step forward into a **right foot forward front stance** (Migi ashi zekutsudachi) and execute a **face/clavicle strike** with the A end of the staff, bringing end A from behind your right shoulder forward. Turning 180 degrees counter-clockwise moving only your left foot ending in a **right foot forward front stance** (Migi ashi zenktsudachi) and perform a **mid-section block** (chuudan uke) with end A passing down next to the right leg and the staff pressing out. Perform a **face/clavicle strike** with end A by having end A pulled back past the right leg in a rowing motion. The left hand should end up by the left hip. **Kiai**.
7) Bring left foot forward into attention stance (Musubidachi) while bringing end B up and execute a upward **chin strike**. End with the staff vertical tucked into your right side with your left hand across your chest 1/3 the way down the B end and your right hand down by your right side 1/3 the way up the A end. End A should be pointing at the ground and end B should be straight up.

# Kihon Kata Nidan - Bo

# Second Basic Bo Form

Start from the **ready stance** (Hidari ashi zenkutsudachi – at position A).

1) Move your left hand from the **lower knifehand block** (Hidari te gedan shuto uke) position over the head to grab the bo staff 1/3 the way down from the B side.

2) Step forward into a **right foot front stance** (Migi ashi zenkutsudachi) then bring the A side of the bo in the right hand in a rowing motion from back to front ending in a **upper face/clavicle strike** with the A side of the bo. The left hand should end up by your left hip.

3) Spin the staff on the vertical plane on the left side of your body. Do this by sliding the right hand down the staff to your left hand, grip with the right hand and slid the left hand to where the right hand was previously positioned.

The staff should end up parallel to the ground at the middle of upper arm height with the A side by your left shoulder and the B side in front of you.

Step forward into a **left foot forward front stance** (Hidari ashi zenkutsudachi) and execute a **horizontal strike** with the A side of the staff. The staff should end up parallel to the ground at the middle of upper arm height with the B side at your right shoulder and the A side pointing forward.

4) Spin the staff on the vertical plane on the right side of your body. Do this by sliding the left hand down the staff to you right hand, grip with the left hand and slide the right hand to where the left hand was previously positioned.

The staff should end up parallel to the ground at the middle of upper arm height with the A side by your shoulder and the B side in front of you.

Step forward into a **right foot forward front stance** (Migi ashi zenktsudachi) and execute a **horizontal strike** with the A side of the staff. The staff should end up parallel to the ground at the middle of upper arm height with the B side by your left shoulder and the A side in front of you.

Step up into a **right leg one-legged stance** (Migi ashi ippon ashidachi) and look to your left while bringing your right hand to your chest and executing a **low section block** (Gedan uke) to your left with the B side.

Chamber the A side high in line with the block.

Step down into **a left foot forward offensive straddle stance** (Hidari ashi kougeki shikodachi), maintaining the chamber of the bo.

Execute a **low section poke** with the B side of the bo.

Step up into a **left leg one-legged stance** (Hidari ashi ippon ashidachi) with a **middle section block** (Chudan uke) to the side with the A side toward the ground and the B side above the head.

Staying in **one-legged stance** (Ippon ashidachi) pivot 90 degrees to your right.

Land in a **right foot forward front stance** (Migi ashi zenktsudachi), maintaining the block.

Execute a **clavicle/face strike** with the A end by bringing the A end down by the right leg in a rowing motion.

5) Execute an **upper chin strike** with the B end of the staff, the A end will end up on your left shoulder.

Begin to row the bo, pulling the B end back with your left hand.

Strike first with the A end of the bow.

Continue to row the bo and strike with the B end of the bo.

Finish the rowing motion with a **clavicle/face strike** with the A end.

6) Look to the front and chamber the bo by pulling your right hand against the body and projecting the B end towards the front.

Moving the right foot, step in to a **right foot forward offensive straddle stance** (Migi ashi kougeki shikodachi) towards the front. Execute a **horizontal strike** with the A end of the staff with the staff ending up chest high, parallel to your body and the floor.

**Side view**

Keeping the left leg steady, bring the right leg back and chamber the bo by bringing the center to your chest.

**Side view**

Kihon Kata Nidan - Bo

**Side view**

Slide the right foot back out into a **right foot forward offensive straddle stance** (Migi ashi kougeki shikodachi) and execute a **mid-section poke** with the A end of the staff. **Kiai.** The B side of the staff should be tucked tightly under your left arm with the staff parallel to the ground.

Move your left foot and turn 180 degrees counter-clockwise to face the rear in a **right foot forward front stance** (Migi ashi zenkutsudachi) and perform a **mid-section block** (Chuudan uke) with end A passing down next to the right leg and the staff pressing out.

**Side view**

Perform a **face/clavicle strike** with end A by having end A pulled back past the right leg in a rowing motion. The left hand should end up by the left hip.

7) Spin the staff on the vertical plane on the left side of your body. Do this by sliding the right hand down the staff to your left hand, grip with the right hand and slid the left hand to where the right hand was previously positioned.

The staff should end up parallel to the ground at the middle of upper arm height with the A side by your left shoulder and the B side in front of you.

Step forward into a **left foot forward front stance** (Hidari ashi zenkutsudachi) and execute a **horizontal strike** with the A side of the staff. The staff should end up parallel to the ground at the middle of upper arm height with the B side at your right shoulder and the A side pointing forward.

8) Spin the staff on the vertical plane on the right side of your body. Do this by sliding the left hand down the staff to you right hand, grip with the left hand and slide the right hand to where the left hand was previously positioned.

Kihon Kata Nidan - Bo

The staff should end up parallel to the ground at the middle of upper arm height with the A side by your shoulder and the B side in front of you.

Step forward into a **right foot forward front stance** (Migi ashi zenktsudachi) and execute a **horizontal strike** with the A side of the staff. The staff should end up parallel to the ground at the middle of upper arm height with the B side by your left shoulder and the A side in front of you.

Keeping the left leg steady, bring the right leg back and chamber the bo by bringing the center to your chest.

Slide the right foot back out into a **right foot forward offensive straddle stance** (Migi ashi kougeki shikodachi) and execute a **mid-section poke** with the A end of the staff. **Kiai.** The B side of the staff should be tucked tightly under your left arm with the staff parallel to the ground.

Move your left foot and turn 180 degrees counter-clockwise to face the front in a **right foot forward front stance** (Migi ashi zenkutsudachi) and perform a **mid-section block** (Chuudan uke) with end A passing down next to the right leg and the staff pressing out.

Perform a **face/clavicle strike** with end A by having end A pulled back past the right leg in a rowing motion. The left hand should end up by the left hip.

9) Bring left foot forward into **attention stance** (Musubidachi) while bringing end B up and execute a upward **chin strike**.

End with the staff vertical tucked into your right side with your left hand across your chest 1/3 the way down the B end and your right hand down by your right side 1/3 the way up the A end. End A should be pointing at the ground and end B should be straight up.

On the command yame move your left hand in a circular knifehand block (Shuto uke). End with the hand down at your left side.

Kihon Kata Nidan - Bo

Students testing for 2<sup>nd</sup> kyu brown belt must
know the form Kihon Kata Nidan - Bo.

E

C | A | D

B

**Kihon Kata Nidan - Bo: Second Basic Bo Form**

**Counts:**
1) Move your left hand from the **lower knifehand block** (Hidari te gedan shuto uke) position over the head to grab the bo staff 1/3 the way down from the B side.
2) Step forward into a **right foot front stance** (Migi ashi zenkutsudachi) then bring the A side of the bo in the right hand in a rowing motion from back to front ending in a **upper face/clavicle strike** with the A side of the bo. The left hand should end up by your left hip.
3) Spin the staff on the vertical plane on the left side of your body. Do this by sliding the right hand down the staff to your left hand, grip with the right hand and slid the left hand to where the right hand was previously positioned. The staff should end up parallel to the ground at shoulder height with the A side by your left shoulder and the B side in front of you. Step forward into a **left foot forward front stance** (Hidari ashi zenkutsudachi) and execute a **horizontal strike** with the A side of the staff. The staff should end up parallel to the ground at shoulder height with the B side at your right shoulder and the A side pointing forward.
4) Spin the staff on the vertical plane on the right side of your body. Do this by sliding the left hand down the staff to you right hand, grip with the left hand and slide the right hand to where the left hand was previously positioned. The staff should end up parallel to the ground at shoulder height with the A side by your shoulder and the B side in front of you. Step forward into a **right foot forward front stance** (Migi ashi zenktsudachi) and execute a **horizontal strike** with the A side of the staff. The staff should end up parallel to the ground at shoulder height with the B side by your left shoulder and the A side in front of you. Step up into a **right leg one-legged stance** (Migi ashi ippon ashidachi) and look to your left while bringing your right hand to your chest and executing a **low section block** (Gedan uke) to your left with the B side. Chamber the A side high in line with the block. Step down into **a left foot forward offensive straddle stance** (Hidari ashi kougeki shikodachi), maintaining the chamber of the bo. Execute a **low section poke** with the B side of the bo. Step up into a **left leg one-legged stance** (Hidari ashi ippon ashidachi) with a **middle section block** (Chudan uke) to the side with the A side toward the ground and the B side above the head. Staying in **one-legged stance** (Ippon ashidachi) pivot 90 degrees to your right. Land in a **right foot forward front stance** (Migi ashi zenktsudachi), maintaining the block. Execute a **clavicle/face strike** with the A end by bringing the A end down by the right leg in a rowing motion.
5) Execute an **upper chin strike** with the B end of the staff, the A end will end up on your left shoulder. Begin to row the bo, pulling the B end back with your left hand. Strike first with the A end of the bow. Continue to row the bo and strike with the B end of the bo. Finish the rowing motion with a **clavicle/face strike** with the A end.
6) Look to the front and chamber the bo by pulling your right hand against the body and projecting the B end towards the front. Moving the right foot, step in to a **right foot forward offensive straddle stance** (Migi ashi kougeki shikodachi) towards the front. Execute a **horizontal strike** with the A end of the staff with the staff ending up chest high, parallel to your body and the floor. Keeping the left leg steady, bring the right leg back and chamber the bo by bringing the center to your chest. Slide the right foot back out into a **right foot forward offensive straddle stance** (Migi ashi kougeki shikodachi) and execute a **mid-section poke** with the A end of the staff. **Kiai**. The B side of the staff

should be tucked tightly under your left arm with the staff parallel to the ground. Move your left foot and turn 180 degrees counter-clockwise to face the rear in a **right foot forward front stance** (Migi ashi zenkutsudachi) and perform a **mid-section block** (Chuudan uke) with end A passing down next to the right leg and the staff pressing out. Perform a **face/clavicle strike** with end A by having end A pulled back past the right leg in a rowing motion. The left hand should end up by the left hip.

7) Spin the staff on the vertical plane on the left side of your body. Do this by sliding the right hand down the staff to your left hand, grip with the right hand and slid the left hand to where the right hand was previously positioned. The staff should end up parallel to the ground at shoulder height with the A side by your left shoulder and the B side in front of you. Step forward into a **left foot forward front stance** (Hidari ashi zenkutsudachi) and execute a **horizontal strike** with the A side of the staff. The staff should end up parallel to the ground at shoulder height with the B side at your right shoulder and the A side pointing forward.

8) Spin the staff on the vertical plane on the right side of your body. Do this by sliding the left hand down the staff to you right hand, grip with the left hand and slide the right hand to where the left hand was previously positioned. The staff should end up parallel to the ground at shoulder height with the A side by your shoulder and the B side in front of you. Step forward into a **right foot forward front stance** (Migi ashi zenktsudachi) and execute a **horizontal strike** with the A side of the staff. The staff should end up parallel to the ground at shoulder height with the B side by your left shoulder and the A side in front of you. Keeping the left leg steady, bring the right leg back and chamber the bo by bringing the center to your chest. Slide the right foot back out into a right foot forward offensive straddle stance (Migi ashi kougeki shikodachi) and execute a mid-section poke with the A end of the staff. **Kiai**. The B side of the staff should be tucked tightly under your left arm with the staff parallel to the ground. Move your left foot and turn 180 degrees counter-clockwise to face the front in a **right foot forward front stance** (Migi ashi zenkutsudachi) and perform a **mid-section block** (Chuudan uke) with end A passing down next to the right leg and the staff pressing out. Perform a **face/clavicle strike** with end A by having end A pulled back past the right leg in a rowing motion. The left hand should end up by the left hip

9) Bring left foot forward into **attention stance** (Musubidachi) while bringing end B up and execute a upward **chin strike**. End with the staff vertical tucked into your right side with your left hand across your chest 1/3 the way down the B end and your right hand down by your right side 1/3 the way up the A end. End A should be pointing at the ground and end B should be straight up.

# Kihon Kata Sandan - Bo

# Third Basic Bo Form

Start from the **ready stance** (Hidari ashi zenkutsudachi – at position A).

1) Move your left hand from the **lower knifehand block** (Hidari te gedan shuto uke) position over the head to grab the bo staff 1/3 the way down from the B side.

2) Step forward into a **right foot front stance** (Migi ashi zenkutsudachi) then bring the A side of the bo in the right hand in a rowing motion from back to front ending in a **upper face/clavicle strike** with the A side of the bo. The left hand should end up by your left hip.

Step up into **attention stance** (Musubidachi) while bringing end B up and execute a **upward chin strike** ending with the staff vertical. Look to your left.

3) As you begin to move, change your grip- left first, then right.

Step up into a **right foot one-legged stance** (Migi ashi ippon ashidachi) and bring your staff out to a 45 degree **mid-section block** to the left side with your left hand on the B side pointing down and the A side in your right hand over your head.

Staying in **one-legged stance** (Ippon ashidachi), pivot 90 degrees to the left.

Land into a **left foot forward front stance** (Hidari ashi zenkutsudachi).

Bring the B side of the bo down past your leg in a rowing motion from back to forward ending in a **upper face/clavicle strike** with the B side of the bo.

Kihon Kata Sandan - Bo

4) Execute an **upper chin strike** with the A end of the staff, the B end will end up on your left shoulder.

Begin to row the bo, pulling the A end back with your right hand. Strike first with the B end of the bow.

Continue to row the bo and strike with the A end of the bo.

Finish the rowing motion with a **clavicle/face strike** with the B end.

5) As you begin to move, switch your grip.

Step up into a **left leg one-legged stance** (Hidari ashi ippon ashidachi) and execute a 45 degree **mid-section block** to the right side with your right hand on the A side pointing down and the B side in your left hand over your head. Staying in **one-legged stance** (Ippon ashidachi), pivot 180 degrees clockwise.

Land into a **right foot forward front stance** (Migi ashi zenktusdachi).

Bring the A side of the bo down past your leg in a rowing motion from back to forward ending in a **upper face/clavicle** strike with the A side of the bo.

6) Execute an **upper chin strike** with the B end of the staff, the A end will end up on your left shoulder.

Kihon Kata Sandan - Bo

Begin to row the bo, pulling the B end back with your left hand.

Strike first with the A end of the bow.

Continue to row the bo and strike with the B end of the bo.

Finish the rowing motion with a **clavicle/face strike** with the A end.

7) Look to the front and chamber the bo by pulling your right hand against the body and projecting the B end towards the front.

Moving the right foot, step in to a **right foot forward offensive straddle stance** (Migi ashi kougeki shikodachi) towards the front. Execute a **horizontal strike** with the A end of the staff with the staff ending up chest high, parallel to your body and the floor.

**Side view**

Step back with the right foot into **attention stance** (Musubidachi) with the staff coming to a stop parallel to the ground at belt level.

**Side view**

8) Step your left foot over your right into a **left foot forward scissor stance** (Hidari ashi hasamidachi) and chamber the bo.

Step forward with the right foot into a **right foot forward offensive straddle stance** (Migi ashi kougeki shikodachi) and execute a **mid-section poke** with the A end of the staff. **Kiai**. The B side of the staff should be tucked tightly under your left arm with the staff parallel to the ground.

Step back with the right foot into **attention stance** (Musubidachi) with the staff coming to a stop parallel to the ground at belt level.

9) Step your left foot over your right into a **left foot forward scissor stance** (Hidari ashi hasamidachi) and chamber the bo.

Step forward with the right foot into a **right foot forward offensive straddle stance** (Migi ashi kougeki shikodachi) and execute a **mid-section poke** with the A end of the staff. **Kiai**. The B side of the staff should be tucked tightly under your left arm with the staff parallel to the ground.

Step back with the right foot into **attention stance** (Musubidachi) with the staff coming to a stop parallel to the ground at belt level.

10) Step your left foot over your right into a **left foot forward scissor stance** (Hidari ashi hasamidachi) and chamber the bo.

Step forward with the right foot into a **right foot forward offensive straddle stance** (Migi ashi kougeki shikodachi) and execute a **mid-section poke** with the A end of the staff. **Kiai**. The B side of the staff should be tucked tightly under your left arm with the staff parallel to the ground.

Begin to move the A end of the staff in a counter-clockwise fashion, tracing the path of an mirrored letter J.

Kihon Kata Sandan - Bo

**Side view**

Step back with the right leg crossing over the left into a **right foot forward scissor stance** (Migi ashi hasamidachi) and continue the **hooking sweep** with the A end of the staff.

Finish the hooking sweep, bringing the A end of the staff up and the B end of the staff down. The staff should be in the same plane as your shoulders.

**Side view**

Step back with your left foot into a **right foot forward offensive straddle stance** (Migi ashi kougeki shikodachi) and execute a **downward parallel block**. Continue looking forward.

Moving only your right foot, turn your body 180 degrees clockwise step into a **left foot forward offensive straddle stance** (Hidari ashi kougeki shikodachi), still looking forward. Execute a high **section 45 degree block** to your left with the B side in your left hand low and the A side in your right hand high.

**Side view**

Move the staff to come to a stop parallel to the ground at waist level.

11) Chamber the bo by bringing it up to chest level.

Kihon Kata Sandan - Bo

Moving the right foot, step in to a **right foot forward offensive straddle stance** (Migi ashi kougeki shikodachi) towards the front. Execute a **horizontal strike** with the A end of the staff with the staff ending up chest high, parallel the floor.

Move your left foot and turn 180 degrees counter-clockwise to face the rear in a **right foot forward front stance** (Migi ashi zenkutsudachi) and perform a **mid-section block** (Chuudan uke) with end A passing down next to the right leg and the staff pressing out.

Perform a **face/clavicle strike** with end A by having end A pulled back past the right leg in a rowing motion. The left hand should end up by the left hip.

12) Slide the right foot back into a **transitional stance** as you bring the center of the bo past your center on the left hand side.

**Side view**

Slide the right foot forward into a **transitional stance** (narrow straddle stance) and allow the bo to slide in your hands, **striking** at stomach height with the A end of the staff and gripping so that both of your hands are on the B end of the staff.

**Side view**

Pull your right foot back into **right foot cat stance** (Migi ashi neko ashidachi) and execute a **45 degree mid-section block** (Chuudan uke) while keeping your hands in the same position on the staff. The B end pointing over your head with the A end pointing toward the ground.

**Side view**

Kihon Kata Sandan - Bo

Step back with your right leg to turn clockwise 180 degrees. Bring the staff horizontal over your head with the A end going in a clockwide direction.

**Side view**

13) Chamber the staff at chest height.

Step around to a **right foot forward offensive straddle stance** (Migi ashi kougeki shikodachi) and continue with your **overhead strike**.

Reverse the direction of the **overhead spin**, sending the bo counter-clockwise. Slide your left hand and then your right hand to their original positions.

Moving the right foot, step in to a **right foot forward offensive straddle stance** (Migi ashi kougeki shikodachi) towards the rear. Execute a **horizontal strike** with the A end of the staff with the staff ending up chest high, parallel to the floor.

Bring the B end of the staff down into your armpit, with the A end pointing to your right at a 45 degree angle.

Looking to the left, bring the staff to a stop parallel to the ground at waist level.

Turn your head to the left to look forward and turn your body 90 degrees counter-clockwise by moving your left foot behind you. Begin to execute an **overhead strike** with the A end of the staff going counter-clockwise. Allow the left hand to slide towards the center of the staff.

**Side view**

Kneel down into a **right foot forward sword stance** (Migi ashi iai dachi) and finish the overhead strike with the B end of the staff tucked into your armpit and the A end of the staff pointing to your right at a 45 degree angle. **Kiai**.

14) Stand by bringing the left foot forward into **attention stance** (Musubidachi) while bringing end B up to execute a **upward chin strike**.

End with the staff vertical tucked into your right side with your left hand across your chest 1/3 the way down the B end and your right hand down by your right side 1/3 the way up the A end. End A should be pointing at the ground and end B should be straight up.

On the command yame move your left hand in a circular **knifehand block** (Shuto uke).

End with the hand down at your left side.

Bow, relaxing your right hand grip slightly so that your hand can slide comfortable back up the bo.

Straight your back and bring your right hand to a natural position on the bo.

Kihon Kata Sandan - Bo

Students testing for 1<sup>st</sup> kyu brown belt must know the form Kihon Kata Sandan - Bo.

**Kihon Kata Sandan - Bo: Third Basic Bo Form**

## Counts:

1) Move your left hand from the **lower knifehand block** (Hidari te gedan shuto uke) position over the head to grab the bo staff 1/3 the way down from the B side.

2) Step forward into a **right foot front stance** (Migi ashi zenkutsudachi) then bring the A side of the bo in the right hand in a rowing motion from back to front ending in a **upper face/clavicle strike** with the A side of the bo. The left hand should end up by your left hip. Step up into **attention stance** (Musubidachi) while bringing end B up and execute a **upward chin strike** ending with the staff vertical. Look to your left.

3) As you begin to move, change your grip- left first, then right. Step up into a **right foot one-legged stance** (Migi ashi ippon ashidachi) and bring your staff out to a 45 degree **mid-section block** to the left side with your left hand on the B side pointing down and the A side in your right hand over your head. Staying in **one-legged stance** (Ippon ashidachi), pivot 90 degrees to the left. Land into a **left foot forward front stance** (Hidari ashi zenkutsudachi). Bring the B side of the bo down past your leg in a rowing motion from back to forward ending in a **upper face/clavicle strike** with the B side of the bo.

4) Execute an **upper chin strike** with the A end of the staff, the B end will end up on your left shoulder. Begin to row the bo, pulling the A end back with your right hand. Strike first with the B end of the bow. Continue to row the bo and strike with the A end of the bo. Finish the rowing motion with a **clavicle/face strike** with the B end.

5) As you begin to move, change your grip- left first, then right. Step up into a **left leg one-legged stance** (Hidari ashi ippon ashidachi) and execute a 45 degree **mid-section block** to the right side with your right hand on the A side pointing down and the B side in your left hand over your head. Staying in **one-legged stance** (Ippon ashidachi), pivot 180 degrees clockwise. Land into a **right foot forward front stance** (Migi ashi zenktusdachi). Bring the A side of the bo down past your leg in a rowing motion from back to forward ending in a **upper face/clavicle** strike with the A side of the bo.

6) Execute an **upper chin strike** with the B end of the staff, the A end will end up on your left shoulder. Begin to row the bo, pulling the B end back with your left hand. Strike first with the A end of the bow. Continue to row the bo and strike with the B end of the bo. Finish the rowing motion with a **clavicle/face strike** with the A end.

7) Look to the front and chamber the bo by pulling your right hand against the body and projecting the B end towards the front. Moving the right foot, step in to a **right foot forward offensive straddle stance** (Migi ashi kougeki shikodachi) towards the front. Execute a **horizontal strike** with the A end of the staff with the staff ending up chest high, parallel to your body and the floor. Step back with the right foot into **attention stance** (Musubidachi) with the staff coming to a stop parallel to the ground at belt level.

8) Step your left foot over your right into a **left foot forward scissor stance** (Hidari ashi hasamidachi) and chamber the bo. Step forward with the right foot into a **right foot forward offensive straddle stance** (Migi ashi kougeki shikodachi) and execute a **mid-section poke** with the A end of the staff. **Kiai.** The B side of the staff should be tucked tightly under your left arm with the staff parallel to the ground. Step back with the right foot into **attention stance** (Musubidachi) with the staff coming to a stop parallel to the ground at belt level.

9) Step your left foot over your right into a **left foot forward scissor stance** (Hidari ashi hasamidachi) and chamber the bo. Step forward with the right foot into a **right foot**

**forward offensive straddle stance** (Migi ashi kougeki shikodachi) and execute a **mid-section poke** with the A end of the staff. **Kiai**. The B side of the staff should be tucked tightly under your left arm with the staff parallel to the ground. Step back with the right foot into **attention stance** (Musubidachi) with the staff coming to a stop parallel to the ground at belt level.

10) Step forward with the right foot into a **right foot forward offensive straddle stance** (Migi ashi kougeki shikodachi) and execute a **mid-section poke** with the A end of the staff. **Kiai**. The B side of the staff should be tucked tightly under your left arm with the staff parallel to the ground. Begin to move the A end of the staff in a counter-clockwise fashion, tracing the path of an mirrored letter J. Step back with the right leg crossing over the left into a **right foot forward scissor stance** (Migi ashi hasamidachi) and continue the **hooking sweep** with the A end of the staff. Finish the hooking sweep, bringing the A end of the staff up and the B end of the staff down. The staff should be in the same plane as your shoulders. Step back with your left foot into a **right foot forward offensive straddle stance** (Migi ashi kougeki shikodachi) and execute a **downward parallel block**. Continue looking forward. Moving only your right foot, turn your body 180 degrees clockwise step into a **left foot forward offensive straddle stance** (Hidari ashi kougeki shikodachi), still looking forward. Execute a **high section 45 degree block** to your left with the B side in your left hand low and the A side in your right hand high. Move the staff to come to a stop parallel to the ground at belt level.

11) Chamber the bo by bringing it up to chest level. Moving the right foot, step in to a **right foot forward offensive straddle stance** (Migi ashi kougeki shikodachi) towards the front. Execute a **horizontal strike** with the A end of the staff with the staff ending up chest high, parallel to the floor. Move your left foot and turn 180 degrees counter-clockwise to face the rear in a **right foot forward front stance** (Migi ashi zenkutsudachi) and perform a **mid-section block** (Chuudan uke) with end A passing down next to the right leg and the staff pressing out. Perform a **face/clavicle strike** with end A by having end A pulled back past the right leg in a rowing motion. The left hand should end up by the left hip.

12) Slide the right foot back into a **transitional stance** (narrow straddle stance) as you bring the center of the bo past your center on the left hand side. Slide the right foot forward into a **transitional stance** and allow the bo to slide in your hands, **striking** at stomach height with the A end of the staff and gripping so that both of your hands are on the B end of the staff. Pull your right foot back into **right foot cat stance** (Migi ashi neko ashidachi) and execute a **45 degree mid-section block** (Chuudan uke) while keeping your hands in the same position on the staff. The B end pointing over your head with the A end pointing toward the ground. Step back with your right leg to turn clockwise 180 degrees. Bring the staff horizontal over your head with the A end going in a clockwide direction. Step around to a **right foot forward offensive straddle stance** (Migi ashi kougeki shikodachi) and continue with your **overhead strike**. Bring the B end of the staff down into your armpit, with the A end pointing to your right at a 45 degree angle. Reverse the direction of the **overhead spin**, sending the bo counter-clockwise. Slide your left hand and then your right hand to their original positions. Looking to the left, bring the staff to a stop parallel to the ground at belt level.

13) Chamber the staff at chest height. Moving the right foot, step in to a **right foot forward offensive straddle stance** (Migi ashi kougeki shikodachi) towards the rear. Execute a **horizontal strike** with the A end of the staff with the staff ending up chest high, parallel to the floor. Turn your head to the left to look forward and turn your body 90 degrees counter-clockwise by moving your left foot behind you. Begin to execute an **overhead strike** with the A end of the staff going counter-clockwise. Allow the left hand to slide towards the center of the staff. Kneel down into a **right foot forward sword stance** (Migi ashi iai dachi) and finish the overhead strike with the B end of the staff tucked into your armpit and the A end of the staff pointing to your right at a 45 degree angle. **Kiai**.

14) Stand by bringing the left foot forward into **attention stance** (Musubidachi) while bringing end B up to execute a **upward chin strike**. End with the staff vertical tucked into your right side with your left hand across your chest 1/3 the way down the B end and your right hand down by your right side 1/3 the way up the A end. End A should be pointing at the ground and end B should be straight up.

# Zenshin Kotai - Sai

# Advancing and Retreating - Sai

Start from the **ready stance** (Uchihachiji dachi – at position A).

1) Bring sai to tsuki with the tsume perpendicular to the floor and the monouchi parallel to the floor.

2) Step forward into **a right foot front stance** (Migi ashi zenkutsudachi) and perform a **right hand center punch** (Migi te chuudan jun zuki). **Kiai.**

Chamber the sai over your left shoulder.

Execute a **strike to your opponent's head**, keeping monouchi horizontal.

Flip the sai back to your forearm.

Begin a **scooping block** with the monouchi turned outwards to your right.

Continue the scooping motion in a clockwise direction until the sai is beyond your center.

Continue to move the sai clockwise.

Settle the sai at center with yari pointed slightly backward.

3) Snap the sai to your forearm.

Step forward into a **left foot front stance** (Hidari ashi zenkutsudachi) and perform a **left hand center punch** (Hidari te chuudan jun zuki). **Kiai**.

Chamber the sai over your right shoulder.

Execute a **strike to your opponent's head**, keeping monouchi horizontal.

Flip the sai back to your forearm.

Begin a **scooping block** with the monouchi turned outwards to your left.

Continue the scooping motion in a counter-clockwise direction until the sai is beyond your center.

Settle the sai at center with yari pointed slightly backward.

4) Snap the sai to your forearm.

Step backward into a **right foot front stance** (Migi ashi zenkutsudachi) and perform a **right hand center punch** (Migi te chuudan jun zuki). **Kiai**.

Chamber the sai over your left shoulder.

Execute a **strike to your opponent's head**, keeping monouchi horizontal.

Flip the sai back to your forearm. Begin a **scooping block** with the monouchi turned outwards to your right. Continue the scooping motion in a clockwise direction.

Settle the sai at center with yari pointed slightly backward.

5) Snap the sai to your forearm.

Step backward into a **left foot front stance** (Hidari ashi zenkutsudachi) and perform a **left hand center punch** (Hidari te chuudan jun zuki). **Kiai**.

Chamber the sai over your right shoulder.

Zenshin Kotai - Sai

Execute a **strike to your opponent's head**, keeping monouchi horizontal.

Flip the sai back to your forearm. Begin a **scooping block** with the monouchi turned outwards to your left. Continue the scooping motion in a counter-clockwise direction.

Settle the sai at center with yari pointed slightly backward.

6) Snap the sai to your forearm, then turn your head to look to the right.

Keeping your knees bent, bring your right leg up to meet your left leg and stack the right arm over the left arm.

Step out into a **right foot forward front stance** (Migi ashi zenkutsudachi) and execute a **strike to your opponent's head**, keeping monouchi horizontal.

Flip the sai back to your forearm.

Begin a **scooping block** with the monouchi turned outwards to your right.

Continue the scooping motion in a clockwise direction.

Settle the sai at center with yari pointed slightly backward.

Snap the sai to your forearm.

Execute a **left hand center reverse punch** (Hidari te chuudan gyaku zuki).

Execute a **right hand center punch** (Migi te chuudan jun zuki)

7) Look over your left shoulder.

Keeping your knees bent, bring your left leg up to your right leg and chamber the left hand over the right shoulder.

Step out into a **left foot forward front stance** (Hidari ashi zenkutsudachi) and execute a **strike to your opponent's head**, keeping monouchi horizontal.

Flip the sai back to your forearm.

Begin a **scooping block** with the monouchi turned outwards to your left.

Continue the scooping motion in a counter-clockwise direction.

Settle the sai at center with yari pointed slightly backward.

Snap the sai to your forearm.

Execute a **right hand center reverse punch** (Migi te chuudan gyaku zuki).

Execute a **left hand center punch** (Hidari te chuudan jun zuki).

8) Look over your right shoulder, bring your right leg up into a **left one-legged stance** (Hidari ashi ippon ashidachi) and chamber for a **right hand down block** (Migi te gedan uke).

Execute a **right hand down block** (Migi te gedan uke) with the tsume vertical.

9) Snap the sai to your forearm.

Snap the sai to your forearm and execute a **right foot side kick** (Migi ashi yoko geri).

Rechamber your kick.

Set the right leg down into a **ready stance** (Uchihachijidachi) and look to the left.

10) Bring your left leg up into a **right one-legged stance** (Migi ashi ippon ashidachi) and chamber for a **left hand down block** (Hidari te gedan uke).

Execute a **left hand down block** (Hidari te gedan uke) with the tsume vertical.

Snap the sai to your forearm and execute a **left foot side kick** (Hidari ashi yoko geri).

Rechamber your kick.

Set the left leg down into **a ready stance** (Uchihachijidachi) and look to the front.

Execute a **right hand center punch** (Migi te chuudan zuki). **Kiai**.

Chamber the sai over your left shoulder.

Execute a **strike to your opponent's head**, keeping monouchi horizontal.

Flip the sai back to your forearm. Begin a **scooping block** with the monouchi turned outwards to your right. Continue the scooping motion in a clockwise direction.

Settle the sai at center with yari pointed slightly backward.

11) Snap the sai to your forearm.

Execute a **left hand center punch** (Hidari te chuudan zuki).

Execute a **right hand center punch** (Migi te chuudan zuki).

Execute a **left hand center punch** (Hidari te chuudan zuki). **Kiai**.

Bring the right foot together with the left to **attention stance** (Musubidachi) and finish (yame).

Bow.

Zenshin Kotai - Sai

```
        ┌─────────────────────────────┐
        │  ┌───┐     ┌───┐     ┌───┐   │
        │  │ C ├─────┤ A ├─────┤ D │   │
        │  └───┘     └─┬─┘     └───┘   │
        │              │               │
        │              │               │
        │            ┌─┴─┐             │
        │            │ B │             │
        │            └───┘             │
        └─────────────────────────────┘
```

<u>Students testing for 2<sup>nd</sup> kyu must
know the form Zenshin Kotai - Sai.</u>

**Zenshin Kotai: Advancing and Retreating**

**Counts:**

1)  Start from the **ready stance** (Uchihachiji dachi – at position A). Bring sai to tsuki with the tsume perpendicular to the floor and the monouchi parallel to the floor.

2)  Step forward into **a right foot front stance** (Migi ashi zenkutsudachi) and perform a **right hand center punch** (Migi te chuudan jun zuki). **Kiai.** Chamber the sai over your left shoulder. Execute a **strike to your opponent's head**, keeping monouchi horizontal. Flip the sai back to your forearm. Execute a clockwise **scooping block** with the monouchi turned outwards. Settle the sai at center with yari pointed slightly backward.

3)  Snap the sai to your forearm. Step forward into a **left foot front stance** (Hidari ashi zenkutsudachi) and perform a **left hand center punch** (Hidari te chuudan jun zuki). **Kiai.** Chamber the sai over your right shoulder. Execute a **strike to your opponent's head**, keeping monouchi horizontal. Flip the sai back to your forearm. Execute a counter-clockwise **scooping block** with the monouchi turned outwards. Settle the sai at center with yari pointed slightly backward.

4)  Snap the sai to your forearm. Step backward into a **right foot front stance** (Migi ashi zenkutsudachi) and perform a **right hand center punch** (Migi te chuudan jun zuki). **Kiai.** Chamber the sai over your left shoulder. Execute a **strike to your opponent's head**, keeping monouchi horizontal. Flip the sai back to your forearm. Execute a clockwise **scooping block** with the monouchi turned outwards. Settle the sai at center with yari pointed slightly backward.

5)  Snap the sai to your forearm. Step backward into a **left foot front stance** (Hidari ashi zenkutsudachi) and perform a **left hand center punch** (Hidari te chuudan jun zuki). **Kiai.** Chamber the sai over your right shoulder. Execute a **strike to your opponent's head**, keeping monouchi horizontal. Flip the sai back to your forearm. Execute a counter-clockwise **scooping block** with the monouchi turned outwards. Settle the sai at center with yari pointed slightly backward.

6)  Snap the sai to your forearm, then turn your head to look to the right. Keeping your knees bent, bring your right leg up to meet your left leg and stack the right arm over the left shoulder. Step out into a **right foot forward front** stance (Migi ashi zenkutsudachi) and execute a **strike to your opponent's head**, keeping monouchi horizontal. Flip the sai back to your forearm. Execute a clockwise **scooping block** with the monouchi turned outwards. Settle the sai at center with yari pointed slightly backward. Snap the sai to your forearm. Execute a **left hand center reverse punch** (Hidari te chuudan gyaku zuki). Execute a **right hand center punch** (Migi te chuudan jun zuki)

7)  Look over your left shoulder. Keeping your knees bent, bring your left leg up to your right leg and chamber the left hand over the right shoulder. Step out into a **left foot forward front stance** (Hidari ashi zenkutsudachi) and execute a **strike to your opponent's head**, keeping monouchi horizontal. Flip the sai back to your forearm. Execute a counter-clockwise **scooping block** with the monouchi turned outwards. Settle the sai at center with yari pointed slightly backward. Snap the sai to your forearm.

Execute a **right hand center reverse punch** (Migi te chuudan gyaku zuki). Execute a **left hand center punch** (Hidari te chuudan jun zuki).

8) Look over your right shoulder, bring your right leg up into a **left one-legged stance** (Hidari ashi ippon ashidachi) and chamber for a **right hand down block** (Migi te gedan uke). Execute a **right hand down block** (Migi te gedan uke) with the tsume vertical.

9) Snap the sai to your forearm. Snap the sai to your forearm and execute a **right foot side kick** (Migi ashi yoko geri). Rechamber your kick. Set the right leg down into a **ready stance** (Uchihachijidachi) and look to the left.

10) Bring your left leg up into a **right one-legged stance** (Migi ashi ippon ashidachi) and chamber for a **left hand down block** (Hidari te gedan uke). Execute a **left hand down block** (Hidari te gedan uke) with the tsume vertical. Snap the sai to your forearm and execute a **left foot side kick** (Hidari ashi yoko geri). Rechamber your kick. Set the left leg down into **a ready stance** (Uchihachijidachi) and look to the front. Execute a **right hand center punch** (Migi te chuudan zuki). **Kiai.** Chamber the sai over your left shoulder. Execute a **strike to your opponent's head**, keeping monouchi horizontal. Flip the sai back to your forearm. Execute a clockwise **scooping block** with the monouchi turned outwards. Settle the sai at center with yari pointed slightly backward.

11) Snap the sai to your forearm. Execute a **left hand center punch** (Hidari te chuudan zuki). Execute a **right hand center punch** (Migi te chuudan zuki). Execute a **left hand center punch** (Hidari te chuudan zuki). **Kiai.**

# Shihohai - Sai

# Four Directions - Sai

Start from the **ready stance** (Uchihachiji dachi – at position A).

1) Bring sai to tsuki with the tsume perpendicular to the floor and the monouchi parallel to the floor.

2) Turn your head to the left.

Bring your right foot in to meet your left foot, then step out with the right foot into a **ready stance** (Uchihachiji dachi) turning 90 degrees to your left and execute a **right hand center punch** (Migi te chuudan zuki). **Kiai**.

Chamber the sai over your left shoulder.

Execute a **strike to your opponent's head**, keeping monouchi horizontal.

Flip the sai back to your forearm.

Begin a **scooping block** with the monouchi turned outwards to your right.

Continue the scooping motion in a clockwise direction until the sai is beyond your center.

Settle the sai at center with yari pointed slightly backward.

3) Snap the sai to your forearm, then turn to look to the left.

Bring your left foot in to meet your right foot, then step out with the left foot into a **ready stance** (Uchihachiji dachi) turning 90 degrees to your left and execute a **left hand center punch** (Hidari te chuudan zuki). **Kiai.**

Chamber the sai over your right shoulder.

Execute a **strike to your opponent's head**, keeping monouchi horizontal.

Flip the sai back to your forearm. Execute a **scooping block** with the monouchi turned outwards to your left. Settle the sai at center with yari pointed slightly backward.

4) Snap the sai to your forearm, then turn to look to the left.

Bring your right foot in to meet your left foot, then step out with the right foot into a **ready stance** (Uchihachiji dachi) turning 90 degrees to your left and execute a **right hand center punch** (Migi te chuudan zuki). **Kiai.**

Chamber the sai over your left shoulder.

Execute a **strike to your opponent's head**, keeping monouchi horizontal.

Flip the sai back to your forearm.

Begin a **scooping block** with the monouchi turned outwards to your right.

Continue the scooping motion in a clockwise direction until the sai is beyond your center.

Settle the sai at center with yari pointed slightly backward.

5) Snap the sai to your forearm, then turn to look to the left.

Bring your left foot in to meet your right foot, then step out with the left foot into a **ready stance** (Uchihachiji dachi) turning 90 degrees to your left and execute a **left hand center punch** (Hidari te chuudan zuki). **Kiai.**

Chamber the sai over your right shoulder.

Execute a **strike to your opponent's head**, keeping monouchi horizontal.

Flip the sai back to your forearm.

Execute a **scooping block** with the monouchi turned outwards to your left.

Settle the sai at center with yari pointed slightly backward.

6) Snap the sai to your forearm, then look to the right.

Move your right leg into a **left foot forward scissor stance** (Hidari ashi hasamidachi) and stack the right arm over the left shoulder.

Execute a **strike to your opponent's head**, keeping monouchi horizontal.

Flip the sai back to your forearm.

Execute a **right leg front kick** (Migi ashi mae geri).

Rechamber the kick and land in a **right foot forward front stance** (Migi ashi zenkutsudachi).

Execute a **left hand center reverse punch** (Hidari te chuudan gyaku zuki).

Execute a **right hand center punch** (Migi te chuudan jun zuki).

7) Move your left leg into a **right foot forward scissor stance** (Migi ashi hasamidachi) and stack the left arm over the right shoulder.

Execute a **strike to your opponent's head**, keeping monouchi horizontal.

Flip the sai back to your forearm.

Execute a **left leg front kick** (Hidari ashi mae geri).

Rechamber the kick and land in a **left foot forward front stance** (Hidari ashi zenkutsudachi).

Execute a **right hand center reverse punch** (Migi te chuudan gyaku zuki).

Execute a **left hand center punch** (Hidari te chuudan jun zuki).

8) Look over your right shoulder, bring your right leg up into a **left one-legged stance** (Hidari ashi ippon ashidachi) and chamber for a **right hand down block** (Migi te gedan uke).

Execute a **right hand down block** (Migi te gedan uke) with the tsume vertical.

9) Snap the sai to your forearm.

Snap the sai to your forearm and execute a **right foot side kick** (Migi ashi yoko geri).

Rechamber your kick.

Set the right leg down into a **ready stance** (Uchihachijidachi) and look to the left.

10) Bring your left leg up into a **right one-legged stance** (Migi ashi ippon ashidachi) and chamber for a **left hand down block** (Hidari te gedan uke).

Execute a **left hand down block** (Hidari te gedan uke) with the tsume vertical.

Snap the sai to your forearm and execute a **left foot side kick** (Hidari ashi yoko geri).

Set the left leg down into **a ready stance** (Uchihachijidachi) and look to the front.

11) Look over your right shoulder.

Step with your right foot into a **right foot forward front stance** (Migi ashi zenkutsudachi) towards position E. Stack your right arm over your left shoulder, keeping the left arm straight.

**Side view**

Execute a **strike to your opponent's head**, keeping monouchi horizontal. **Kiai**.

**Side view**

Flip the sai back to your forearm.

**Side view**

Execute a **scooping block** with the monouchi turned outwards to your right. Continue the scooping motion in a clockwise direction. Settle the sai at center with yari pointed slightly backward. Snap the sai to your forearm.

Execute a **left hand center reverse punch** (Hidari te chuudan gyaku zuki).

Execute a **right hand center punch** (Migi te chuudan jun zuki).

12) Step with your right foot into a **right foot forward front stance** (Migi ashi zenkutsudachi) facing forward. Stack your right arm over your left.

Execute a **strike to your opponent's head**, keeping monouchi horizontal. **Kiai.**

Flip the sai back to your forearm.

Execute a **scooping block** with the monouchi turned outwards to your left. Continue the scooping motion in a clockwise direction. Settle the sai at center with yari pointed slightly backward.

Snap the sai to your forearm.

Execute a **left hand center reverse punch** (Hidari te chuudan gyaku zuki).

Execute a **right hand center punch** (Migi te chuudan jun zuki).

Bring your left leg up into a **right one-legged stance** (Migi ashi ippon ashidachi) to block the groin and execute a **two handed backhand block** (Morote haisho uke).

Step out with the left foot into an **offensive straddle stance** (Kougeki shikodachi) and execute a **double down block** (Morote gedan uke). **Kiai**.

Bring the right foot together with the left to **attention stance** (Musubidachi) and finish (yame).

Shihohai - Sai

Students testing for 1<sup>st</sup> kyu must
know the form Shihohai - Sai.

**Shihohai: Four Directions**

## Counts:

1) Start from the **ready stance** (Uchihachiji dachi – at position A). Bring sai to tsuki with the tsume perpendicular to the floor and the monouchi parallel to the floor.

2) Turn your head to the left. Bring your right foot in to meet your left foot, then step out with the right foot into a **ready stance** (Uchihachiji dachi) turning 90 degrees to your left and execute a **right hand center punch** (Migi te chuudan zuki). **Kiai.** Chamber the sai over your left shoulder. Execute a **strike to your opponent's head**, keeping monouchi horizontal. Flip the sai back to your forearm. Execute a clockwise **scooping block** with the monouchi turned outwards. Settle the sai at center with yari pointed slightly backward.

3) Snap the sai to your forearm, then turn to look to the left. Bring your left foot in to meet your right foot, then step out with the left foot into a **ready stance** (Uchihachiji dachi) turning 90 degrees to your left and execute a **left hand center punch** (Hidari te chuudan zuki). **Kiai.** Chamber the sai over your right shoulder. Execute a **strike to your opponent's head**, keeping monouchi horizontal. Flip the sai back to your forearm. Execute a counter-clockwise **scooping block** with the monouchi turned outwards. Settle the sai at center with yari pointed slightly backward.

4) Snap the sai to your forearm, then turn your head to the left. Bring your right foot in to meet your left foot, then step out with the right foot into a **ready stance** (Uchihachiji dachi) turning 90 degrees to your left and execute a **right hand center punch** (Migi te chuudan zuki). **Kiai.** Chamber the sai over your left shoulder. Execute a **strike to your opponent's head**, keeping monouchi horizontal. Flip the sai back to your forearm. Execute a clockwise **scooping block** with the monouchi turned outwards. Settle the sai at center with yari pointed slightly backward.

5) Snap the sai to your forearm, then turn to look to the left. Bring your left foot in to meet your right foot, then step out with the left foot into a **ready stance** (Uchihachiji dachi) turning 90 degrees to your left and execute a **left hand center punch** (Hidari te chuudan zuki). **Kiai.** Chamber the sai over your right shoulder. Execute a **strike to your opponent's head**, keeping monouchi horizontal. Flip the sai back to your forearm. Execute a counter-clockwise **scooping block** with the monouchi turned outwards. Settle the sai at center with yari pointed slightly backward.

6) Snap the sai to your forearm, then look to the right. Move your right leg into a **left foot forward scissor stance** (Hidari ashi hasamidachi) and stack the right arm over the left shoulder. Execute a **strike to your opponent's head**, keeping monouchi horizontal. Flip the sai back to your forearm. Execute a **right leg front kick** (Migi ashi mae geri). Rechamber the kick and land in a **right foot forward front stance** (Migi ashi zenkutsudachi). Execute a **left hand center reverse punch** (Hidari te chuudan gyaku zuki). Execute a **right hand center punch** (Migi te chuudan jun zuki).

7) Move your left leg into a **right foot forward scissor stance** (Migi ashi hasamidachi) and stack the left arm over the right shoulder. Execute a **strike to your opponent's head**, keeping monouchi horizontal. Flip the sai back to your forearm. Execute a **left leg front kick** (Hidari ashi mae geri). Rechamber the kick and land in a **left foot forward front**

**stance** (Hidari ashi zenkutsudachi). Execute a **right hand center reverse punch** (Migi te chuudan gyaku zuki). Execute a **left hand center punch** (Hidari te chuudan jun zuki).

8) Look over your right shoulder, bring your right leg up into a **left one-legged stance** (Hidari ashi ippon ashidachi) and chamber for a **right hand down block** (Migi te gedan uke). Execute a **right hand down block** (Migi te gedan uke) with the tsume vertical.

9) Snap the sai to your forearm and execute a **right foot side kick** (Migi ashi yoko geri). Rechamber your kick. Set the right leg down into a **ready stance** (Uchihachijidachi) and look to the left.

10) Bring your left leg up into a **right one-legged stance** (Migi ashi ippon ashidachi) and chamber for a **left hand down block** (Hidari te gedan uke). Execute a **left hand down block** (Hidari te gedan uke) with the tsume vertical. Snap the sai to your forearm and execute a **left foot side kick** (Hidari ashi yoko geri). Set the left leg down into **a ready stance** (Uchihachijidachi) and look to the front.

11) Look over your right shoulder. Step with your right foot into a **right foot forward front stance** (Migi ashi zenkutsudachi) towards position E. Stack your right arm over your left shoulder. Execute a **strike to your opponent's head**, keeping monouchi horizontal. **Kiai**. Flip the sai back to your forearm. Execute a clockwise **scooping block** with the monouchi turned outwards. Settle the sai at center with yari pointed slightly backward. Snap the sai to your forearm. Execute a **left hand center reverse punch** (Hidari te chuudan gyaku zuki). Execute a **right hand center punch** (Migi te chuudan jun zuki).

12) Step with your right foot into a **right foot forward front stance** (Migi ashi zenkutsudachi) facing forward. Stack your right arm over your left shoulder. Execute a **strike to your opponent's head**, keeping monouchi horizontal. **Kiai**. Flip the sai back to your forearm. Execute a clockwise **scooping block** with the monouchi turned outwards. Settle the sai at center with yari pointed slightly backward. Snap the sai to your forearm. Execute a **left hand center reverse punch** (Hidari te chuudan gyaku zuki). Execute a **right hand center punch** (Migi te chuudan jun zuki). Bring your left leg up into a **right one-legged stance** (Migi ashi ippon ashidachi) to block the groin and execute a **two handed backhand block** (Morote haisho uke). Step out with the left foot into an **offensive straddle stance** (Kougeki shikodachi) and execute a **double down block** (Morote gedan uke). **Kiai**.

# Rho Hai Sho - Sai

# Vision of a Crane Minor - Sai

Start from the **ready stance** (Uchihachiji dachi – at position A).

1) Bring sai to tsuki with the tsume perpendicular to the floor and the monouchi parallel to the floor.

2) Turn your head to the left.

Step forward with the right leg towards C into a **sword stance** (Iai dachi) and execute a **lower crosshand block** (Gedan juji uke) with the tsume vertical. **Kiai**.

3) Step up, keeping the knees bent, and bring the sai up to perform a double forearm block.

Step out with the right leg on a 45° angle towards D into a **right foot forward offensive straddle stance** (Migi ashi kougeki shikodachi). Execute a **double shoulder punch** (Morote kata zuki), facing towards the right.

4) Extend the left hand forward to grab, having the tsume vertical.

Step forward with your right foot into a **right foot forward offensive straddle stance** (Migi ashi kougeki shikodachi) and strike your outstretched hand with an **elbow strike** (Embi).

Step back with the right foot into a **left foot forward scissor stance** (Hidari ashi hasamidachi) and chamber the right hand under the left.

188

**Side view**

Open both sai to execute a **right hand lower block** (Migi te gedan uke) and **left hand upper block** (Hidari te jodan uke). Keep the sai in line with eachother and the tsume vertical.

5) Flip both sai back to your forearms and step forward with right foot into **right foot forward offensive straddle stance** (Hidari ashi kougeki shikodachi) and stack the left arm under the right.

Step back with the right foot into **left foot forward scissor stance** (Hidari ashi hasamidachi) and open both sai to execute a **left hand lower block** (Hidari te gedan uke) and a **right hand upper block** (Migi te jodan uke). Keep the sai in line with eachother and the tsume vertical.

Flip both sai back and push the left foot back into a **right foot forward front stance** (Migi ashi zenkutsudachi) and chamber for **right hand down block** (Migi te gedan uke).

**Side view**

Execute a **right hand down block** (Migi te gedan uke).

Bring the left foot in to meet the right foot and push back towards the front into a **left foot forward front stance** (Hidari ashi zenkutsudachi) while swinging the right hand up and around.

Execute a **left center punch** (Hidari te chuudan jun zuki).

6) Step forward with the right foot into a **right foot forward front stance** (Migi ashi zenkutsudachi) and execute a **right hand chasing punch** (Migi te oizuki).

Step forward with the left leg into **a left foot forward front stance** (Hidari ashi zenkutsudachi).

Twist into **a left foot forward defensive straddle stance** (Hidari ashi boubi shikodachi) and execute a **left shoulder punch** (Hidari te kata zuki). **Kiai**.

Draw the left foot back into a **left foot forward cat stance** (Hidari ashi neko ashidachi) and execute a **right hand upper block** (Migi te jodan uke) and a **left hand lower palm heel block** (Hidari te gedan shote uke).

**Side view**

7) Turn into a **left foot forward scissor stance** (Hidari ashi hasamidachi) as you simultaneously open the sai to execute a **strike to the temple**.

**Side view**

Flip the sai back to your forearm.

Execute a **right foot front kick** (Migi ashi mae geri).

Rho Hai Sho - Sai

Rechamber your kick.

Land forward and step into a **right foot forward scissor stance** (Migi ashi hasamidachi) as you simultaneously execute a fast **right lower block** (Migi te gedan uke) with the monouchi turned out.

Execute a fast **left lower block** (Hidari te gedan uke).

Leaving the left hand in place, execute a second **right lower block** (Migi te gedan uke) slowly with tension to form a **lower backhand cross block** (Gedan haisho juji uke).

8) Step back with the left foot into a **right foot forward offensive straddle stance** (Migi ashi kougeki shikodachi) and pull both hands to the right axila with the backs of the hands touching and the monouchi horizontal.

Execute a **right hand shoulder punch** (Migi te chuudan zuki).

**Side view**

Swing the right around across to face the rear, position A.

Execute a **left hand shoulder punch** (Hidari te kata zuki).

Step through with the right leg towards the rear of the room into a **right foot forward offensive straddle stance** (Migi ashi kougeki shikodachi) and execute a **right shoulder punch** (Migi te kata zuki).

Bring the left foot in to meet the right and push it towards the front of the room to end in a **left foot forward front stance** (Hidari ashi zenkutsudachi) and swing the right arm across to face front.

Execute a **left hand center punch** (Hidari te chuudan jun zuki).

9) Execute a **right hand reverse center punch** (Migi te chuudan gyaku zuki).

Execute a **left hand center punch** (Hidari te chuudan jun zuki). **Kiai**.

Bring your right leg up into a **left one-legged stance** (Hidari ashi ippon ashidachi) to block the groin and execute a **two handed backhand block** (Morote haisho uke).

Step out with the right foot into an **offensive straddle stance** (Kougeki shikodachi) and execute a **double down block** (Morote gedan uke). **Kiai**.

Bring the right foot together with the left to **attention stance** (Musubidachi) and finish (yame).

Bow.

Rho Hai Sho - Sai

Students testing for Shodan must
know the form Rho Hai Sho - Sai.

**Rho Hai Sho: Vision of a Crane Minor**

**Counts:**
1) Bring sai to tsuki with the tsume perpendicular to the floor and the monouchi parallel to the floor.
2) Turn your head to the left. Step forward with the right leg towards C into a **sword stance** (Iai dachi) and execute a **lower crosshand block** (Gedan juji uke) with the tsume vertical. **Kiai.**
3) Step up, keeping the knees bent, and bring the sai up to perform a double forearm block. Step out with the right leg on a 45° angle towards D into a **right foot forward offensive straddle stance** (Migi ashi kougeki shikodachi). Execute a **double shoulder punch** (Morote kata zuki), facing towards the right.
4) Extend the left hand forward to grab, having the tsume vertical. Step forward with your right foot into a **right foot forward offensive straddle stance** (Migi ashi kougeki shikodachi) and strike your outstretched hand with an **elbow strike** (Embi). Step back with the right foot into a **left foot forward scissor stance** (Hidari ashi hasamidachi) and chamber the right hand under the left. Open both sai to execute a **right hand lower block** (Migi te gedan uke) and **left hand upper block** (Hidari te jodan uke). Keep the sai in line with eachother and the tsume vertical.
5) Flip both sai back to your forearms and step forward with right foot into **right foot forward offensive straddle stance** (Hidari ashi kougeki shikodachi) and stack the left arm under the right. Step back with the right foot into **left foot forward scissor stance** (Hidari ashi hasamidachi) and open both sai to execute a **left hand lower block** (Hidari te gedan uke) and a **right hand upper block** (Migi te jodan uke). Keep the sai in line with eachother and the tsume vertical. Flip both sai back and push the left foot back into a **right foot forward front stance** (Migi ashi zenkutsudachi) and chamber for **right hand down block** (Migi te gedan uke). Execute a **right hand down block** (Migi te gedan uke). Bring the left foot in to meet the right foot and push back towards the front into a **left foot forward front stance** (Hidari ashi zenkutsudachi) while swinging the right hand up and around. Execute a **left center punch** (Hidari te chuudan jun zuki).
6) Step forward with the right foot into a right foot forward front stance (Migi ashi zenkutsudachi) and execute a **right hand chasing punch** (Migi te oizuki). Step forward with the left leg into **a left foot forward front stance** (Hidari ashi zenkutsudachi). Twist into **a left foot forward defensive straddle stance** (Hidari ashi boubi shikodachi) and execute a **left shoulder punch** (Hidari te kata zuki). **Kiai.** Draw the left foot back into a **left foot forward cat stance** (Hidari ashi neko ashidachi) and execute a **right hand upper block** (Migi te jodan uke) and a **left hand lower palm heel block** (Hidari te gedan shote uke).
7) Turn into a **left foot forward scissor stance** (Hidari ashi hasamidachi) as you simultaneously open the sai to execute a **strike to the temple**. Flip the sai back to your forearm. Execute a **right foot front kick** (Migi ashi mae geri). Land forward and step into a **right foot forward scissor stance** (Migi ashi hasamidachi) as you simultaneously execute a fast **right lower block** (Migi te gedan uke) with the monouchi turned out.

Execute a fast **left lower block** (Hidari te gedan uke). Leaving the left hand in place, execute a second **right lower block** (Migi te gedan uke) slowly with tension to form a **lower backhand cross block** (Gedan haisho juji uke).

8) Step back with the left foot into a **right foot forward offensive straddle stance** (Migi ashi kougeki shikodachi) and pull both hands to the right axila with the backs of the hands touching and the monouchi horizontal. Execute a **right hand shoulder punch** (Migi te kata zuki). Swing the right around across to face the rear, position A. Execute a **left hand shoulder punch** (Hidari te kata zuki). Step through with the right leg towards the rear of the room into a **right foot forward offensive straddle stance** (Migi ashi kougeki shikodachi) and execute a **right shoulder punch** (Migi te kata zuki). Bring the left foot in to meet the right and push it towards the front of the room to end in a **left foot forward front stance** (Hidari ashi zenkutsudachi) and swing the right arm across to face front. Execute a **left hand center punch** (Hidari te chuudan jun zuki).

9) Execute a **right hand reverse center punch** (Migi te chuudan gyaku zuki). Execute a **left hand center punch** (Hidari te chuudan jun zuki). **Kiai**. Bring your right leg up into a **left one-legged stance** (Hidari ashi ippon ashidachi) to block the groin and execute a **two handed backhand block** (Morote haisho uke). Step out with the right foot into an **offensive straddle stance** (Kougeki shikodachi) and execute a **double down block** (Morote gedan uke). **Kiai**.

# Kobudo

## History

Kobudo generally refers to the classical weapons traditions of Okinawan Martial Arts. The Bo, Sai, Tonfa, Kama, and Nunchaku are the most common but there are other weapons including the paddle (Eku), some brass knuckle type weapons design to make the fist heavier and protect it (Tekko), a short spear (Tinpe) and shield (Rochin), and a weighted chain (Suruchin).

Many weapons were developed from common objects that would be available to the general populace, as weapons were banned on several occasions. These objects were chosen because of their versatility like the bo or portability and discretion such as the nunchaku which could be concealed in a pouch or suruchin which would fit in a pocket. These were weapons that could still be carried during these bans unlike the katana or naginata.

There were two great turning points in the history of the Okinawan martial arts. The first was the 'Order of the Sword Hunt' implemented by King Shoshin (1477-1526), by which the carrying of weapons was prohibited for not only the general public but the warrior class as well. The second was the 'Policy of Banning Weapons' enforced after the Satsuma Invasion in 1609. The Okinawans naturally began to think of ways to defend themselves and their property using ordinary tools or farm equipment. They discovered that they could fight against swords or spears on the same footing using such tools. As they kept studying and making inventions, they devised Okinawa's martial arts including weaponry. Yoshukai training includes learning the traditional weapons including nunchaku, bo, sai, tonfa, and katana. Other traditional Okinawan weapons include the kama, surujin, and eku.

## Nunchaku

A nunchaku is composed of two sections of wood (or metal in modern incarnations) connected by a cord or chain. There is much controversy over its origins: some say it was originally a Chinese weapon, others say it evolved from a threshing flail, while one theory purports that it was developed from a horse's bit or Muge. Chinese nunchaku tend to be rounded, whereas Japanese versions are octagonal, and they were originally linked by horse hair. There are many variations on the nunchaku, ranging from the three section

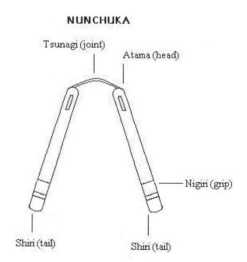

staff (san-setsu-kon nunchaku), to smaller multi-section nunchaku. The nunchaku are relatively small and easy to carry and conceal.

Yoshukai nunchaku kata include:
Kihon Kata (Basic Form)
Kihon Kata Shodan (First Basic Form)
Yoshu (Constant Improvement)
Yoshu Dai (Upper Constant Improvement)

Components of the nunchaku are:
Shiri – Tail, the ends of the nunchaku past the grip
Nigiri – Grip, about 2" from the ends of each section
Atama – Head, the tops of each section where the cord attaches
Tsunagi – Joint, the cord or chain connection


Bo

The bo is a six-foot staff, sometimes tapered at either end. It was perhaps developed from a farming tool called a tenbin (a stick placed across the shoulders with baskets or sacks hanging from either end), the handle to a rake or a shovel; or from walking sticks used by travelers, especially monks. The bo has no edge or shaft so all of it is used. Some of the techniques for the bo are nagi (mowing down), tsuki (punching or poking), and utsu (striking).

Yoshukai bo kata include:
Kihon Kata Shodan (First Basic Form)
Kihon Kata Nidan (Second Basic Form)
Kihon Kata Sandan (Third Basic Form)
Shounnokon

The parts of the bo are:
Shin – Center
Kata – Shoulder (area around the shin)
Monouchi – Striking area, comprising the majority of the length of the bo
Yari – Point

BO

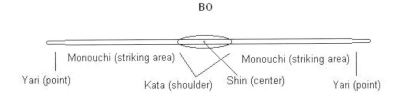

## Sai

The sai appears similar to a short sword, but is not bladed and the end is traditionally blunt. The sai is sometimes believed to be a variation on a tool used to create furrows in the ground. Records from China show its original existence in a much more elongated form where it was known as Tsai and was used purely as a weapon. The weapon is metal and of the truncheon class with its length dependent upon the forearm of the user. The two shorter prongs on either side of the main shaft are used for trapping (and sometimes breaking) other weapons such as a sword or bo. The sai originally reached Japan in the form of the jitte or jutte, which has only a single prong. Both are truncheon-like weapons, used for striking and bludgeoning. Sai were thought to be given to those in Okinawan society that the Japanese could trust to maintain order. Sai are traditionally carried in threes, two are used in combat and the third is used as either a precursor to the actual fight and is thrown at the enemy, or as a spare in the event that one is knocked from the hand. There are many other variations on the sai with varying prongs for trapping and blocking, and the monouchi, or shaft, can be round or octagonal. Sai were also used as handcuffs and were a symbol of authority in Okinawa. A form known as nunti sai, sometimes called manji sai has the two shorter prongs pointed in opposite directions, with another monouchi instead of a grip.

Yoshukai sai kata include:
Zen Shin Kotai (Advancing and Retreating)
Shihohai (Four Directions)
Rho Hai Sho (Vision of a Crane Minor)
Rho Hai Dai (Vision of a Crane Major)
Mugen (Infinity)
Bassai (To Breach a Fortress)
Yosei no Kata (Form of Yosei aka Yuki Koda)

The components of the sai are:
Tsukagashira – Head, used for most punching strikes
Nigiri – Grip
Tsume – Nail, the prongs to the side of the main nail
Monouchi – Striking area, the main nail of the weapon except the point
Yari – Point

## Tonfa

The tonfa is more readily recognized by its modern development in the form of the police nightstick, although its usage differs. It supposedly originated as the handle of a millstone used for grinding grain. The tonfa is traditionally made from red oak, and can be gripped by the short perpendicular handle or by the longer main shaft. As with all Okinawan weapons, many of the forms are reflective of "empty hand" techniques.

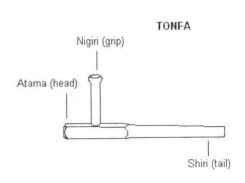

Yoshukai uses the tonfa in:
Tensho (Rolling Palms)

The components of the tonfa are:
Atama – Head, the part usually used for punching
Nigiri – Grip
Shiri – Tail, the end of the longer section used for blocking or striking

## Katana

The katana is a curved sword originating in the Muromachi period in Japan. It was considered the symbol of a samurai. The forging of a Japanese blade typically took hours or days, and was considered a sacred art. As with many complex endeavors, rather than a single craftsman, several artists were involved. There was a smith to forge the rough shape, often a second smith to fold the metal, a specialist polisher, and even a specialist for the edge itself. Often, there were sheath, hilt, and tsuba specialists as well. The sword is made using two steels, one folded more times than the other, or of a lesser carbon content. When both sections have been folded adequately, they are bent into a 'U' shape and the softer piece is inserted into the harder piece, at which point they are hammered out into a long blade shape. By the end of the process, the two pieces of steel are fused together, but retain their differences in hardness. This allows for a hard edge matched with a softer casing to help prevent shattering.

The koshirae is the mounting 'worn' by a katana when it is being worn by its owner. A koshirae should be presented horizontally with the tsuka or hilt to the left, particularly in times of peace with the reason being that you cannot unsheathe the sword easily this way. This is how it should be presented during tournaments or official presentations. Master Yamamoto used a katana to cut 10 centimeters into an actual helmet, which partly motivated the inclusion of the katana in Yoshukai. The sequences used in Yoshukai are derived from iaido, the art of drawing and cutting.

Yoshukai uses the Katana in:
Iai 1-8 (Sword 1-8)

Components of the katana and koshirae are:
Ha – the edge of the blade; typically much stronger than the rest of the blade
Hamon – the pattern on the blade indicating the border between the harder ha and the softer mune
Kashira – butt cap (or pommel) on the end of the hilt
Koiguchi – mouth of the scabbard or its fitting; traditionally made of buffalo horn
Sageo – cord used to tie scabbard to the belt/obi when worn
Same-kawa (samegawa) – ray or shark skin wrapping of the tsuka (handle/hilt)
Saya – a wooden scabbard for the blade; traditionally done in lacquered wood
Tsuba – sword guard
Tsuka – hilt; made of wood and wrapped in samegawa

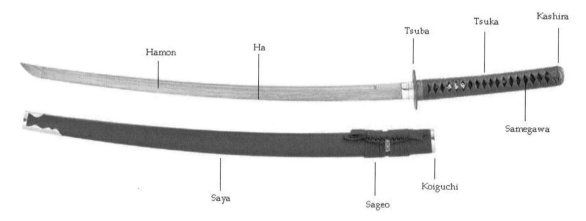

# Fighting

Yoshukai students should expect to spend a significant part of their training developing practical and effective fighting skills, both offensive and defensive. Yoshukai emphasizes solid strikes, kicks and blocks as opposed to techniques that deflect or redirect an opponent's force as in martial arts such as Hapkido, Aikido or Judo. While Yoshukai does teach some techniques from those styles (throws, locks, etc.), particularly in self-defense training and Ippon Kumite, it does not emphasize them in the way that a soft style does. Yoshukai fighting is stand-up fighting only, using blocks, strikes and kicks to incapacitate an opponent, with no emphasis on ground work (grappling or wrestling).

Fighting requires speed, endurance, strength, proper technique and, above all, spirit and heart. Being a good student and fighter also means knowing when *not* to fight. Yoshukai students should be respectful of others and "be prudent in action" at all times. Students should not be drawn easily into fights, and fighting should only be used outside of class when the student is in true danger, and even then only as a last resort. That said, in the event that a student is attacked and cannot otherwise get away, Yoshukai teaches them the skills necessary to respond quickly and efficiently with potentially lethal force.

Beginning students should begin their fighting training with basic instruction on blocks, strikes, and kicks. Fundamental principles regarding guard, fighting stance, and how to safely execute techniques (e.g. striking with the first two knuckles, tucking the thumb) should also be learned before a student begins to spar. Once those basics have been established, students should begin sparring very lightly, focusing on learning how to apply the techniques they have learned, how to attack with combinations, and how to exercise control so as to avoid injury to themselves and others. Training will gradually increase in technical difficult and intensity as students advance in rank.

General Fighting Techniques and Strategy:

Fighting strategy varies greatly depending on what kind of fighting you are doing. A street fight is entirely different from competition fighting like point sparring or even full– or semi-knockdown fighting. However, some general principles and strategy apply across the board.

First of all, fighters should develop a solid *guard*. A fighter's guard refers to the way she positions her hands and arms to protect her face and torso. While a strong guard is key to good defensive and offensive fighting, determining the proper guard position is not always easy and often depends on your opponent and the situation. Fundamentally, good guard position is important because it enables you to protect yourself from an attack to the chest or face with little to no movement, while also keeping your arms in a position where you can easily strike out at your opponent offensively.

Generally speaking a typical guard position involves resting both arms comfortably on your chest (you don't want to waste energy by holding them away from your body if you don't have to) with your forward hand in front of your body at approximately chin level and your back hand wresting against your chin. Your elbows should be fairly close together on your chest so that you minimize your stomach and torso as a target. Some fighters prefer to keep their hands in a closed fist at all times so they are always ready to strike, while others prefer to keep open hands so that they can easily deflect attacks or grab their opponent. If you keep your hands open, your fingers are more vulnerable to attack and injury. Fighters will also often vary the height of their guard based on their opponent. So for instance if you are fighting someone in semi-knockdown fighting where strikes to the head are not allowed and you know that your opponent is not likely to throw a head high kick, you can safely drop your guard lower to protect your torso since your head is an unlikely target. Conversely, if you are fighting an opponent who is taller than you or who is flexible enough for head high kicks, you would probably want to keep a higher guard to avoid dangerous techniques to the head.

Second, fighters should practice movement in their fighting, specifically they should work on moving along diagonals so as to create better opportunities for strikes and kicks, rather than simply moving forward and backwards.

Third, good fighters recognize that to win a fight they will most likely have to sustain some amount of damage in the process. Understanding how to take hits and how to minimize damage to yourself is a crucial part of martial arts training. As such, students should work on body conditioning (e.g. punching/striking a heavy bag without gloves and taking punches to the body).

## Point Sparring

One of the first forms of fighting a Yoshukai student will be exposed to is point sparring. Point sparring is a competition style of fighting in which fighters will attempt to earn points by striking certain parts of an opponent's body. Point sparring is a fun and valuable exercise, but it should not be confused with "real" fighting or self-defense. As will be discussed below, things that would enable you to win in a point sparring match, may not be successful in a self-defense context. Conversely, techniques that would be extremely successful in a self-defense scenario (e.g. strikes to the knee, eye gouges) are proscribed in point sparring. Nevertheless, point sparring is valuable not only as a fun means of competition and exercise, but also as a way of practicing techniques and developing speed, reaction time, and timing.

To begin a point sparring match, students line up facing each other. They bow, and the judge (or instructor) will then say "fighting stance", after which, students step back into a comfortable fighting stance (usually a mae dachi – forward stance) and kiai. The center judge will then explain the rules (see below). In a competition setting, there should be four corner judges and one center judge, all of whom will score the match. Once the rules have been explained, the judge will say "hajime" – meaning "begin" – and the match starts. While some competitors may choose to touch gloves before beginning the fight, the fight has technically started as soon as "hajime" is called and touching gloves is not required.

Point sparring matches are generally very fast paced. Judges will call "point" whenever they see what they think is or might be a qualifying strike. At the call of "point" or "break" opponents will immediately cease fighting and go back to their original starting position. At that point, the center judge will call for judge's decision (hantei), and each judge will indicate either that one of the opponents scored a point or that no point should be awarded. If a point is awarded, the center judge will call out the appropriate score. Regardless of whether a point is scored or not, the center judge will then have the opponents begin again. The match will continue in this fashion until either time has elapsed (each match is usually two minutes) or one opponent has scored the maximum number of points (most matches go to either three or five points). At the end of the round, the center judge will announce the winner, and opponents will bow to each other and the judges and shake hands before leaving the mat.

In competition, opponents will be matched up as much as possible based on age, gender, size and rank. However, depending on the number of competitors, participants may have to fight outside of their rank, gender, or weight class.

Point Sparring Rules:
- A point is awarded for a legitimate strike to the head gear or the torso.
- No strikes are allowed to the face, groin, or especially vulnerable areas such as the throat or joints.
- Hand and foot techniques to the head gear are allowed, but no knees or elbows to the head are allowed.
- At the Yoshukai Traditional Tournament, kicks to the thigh are allowed but *only* if they are followed up by an additional technique. Leg kicks do not earn points, and solitary leg kicks are prohibited.
- With the limited exception of leg kicks followed by an additional technique, all techniques must be above the belt.
- Strikes to the arms are allowed but do not earn points.
- Strikes to the back are discouraged, and direct strikes to the kidneys or spine are not allowed.
- Point sparring should generally be lighter contact fighting showing control and proper technique. Full force should not be used. Similarly, pulled techniques can be scored at the discretion of the judges (e.g. Judges may choose to award a point where one opponent clearly could have struck an opponent in the temple for instance, but pulled the technique just before impact).
- Full gear should be worn at all times, including mouth guard, head and foot gear, and gloves. Men should wear a cup, and a chest protector is optional for women. In Yoshukai, gloves and foot gear should cover the entire hand and foot, fingerless gloves and foot gear that does not cover the toes are discouraged or not allowed at all.
- Opponents who accidentally violate any of these rules will be given a warning, and repeated violations will result in disqualification or forfeiture. Intentional violators may be disqualified immediately.
- If an opponent falls or goes outside of the ring, opponents will be ordered to stop (matte) and will be reset in the center before beginning again.

Point Sparring Strategy:
It is important to remember that point sparring is very different from a "real" fight or full contact fighting. Because opponents are separated each time a point is (or could possibly be) scored, speed is essential. Fundamentally, what matters is being the first to score a hit. Thus, in point sparring if you lunge for an attack and strike first, you could easily win a point even though your opponent might strike seconds later. In a self-defense situation or in full contact fighting, a student has to think equally about defense as well as offense, but in point sparring a more offensive fighter is likely to have an advantage over

someone who fights more defensively.  Put another way, point sparring focuses on the short game, where as full contact fighting focuses on a longer fight where a competitor's success will be gauged based on the entire fight rather than on how quickly he could score a single hit on his opponent.

One point sparring strategy is for students to think about zones or ranges of attack.  For instance, when competitors have five or six feet of distance between them they are in a zone where neither can easily attack.  This is a relative safe zone.  Moving closer by a foot or so, competitors enter an intermediate range where opponents can attack but will still have to close some distance.  The final range (approximately 1-2 feet away) is essentially the attack zone, where the first person to attack is the one who is likely to score the point.  Students should be conscious of how close or how far apart they are from each other, and once they are in the "attack zone" they should attack immediately.

Additionally, in point sparring a fighter should position their body such that their torso is turned away from their opponent by standing with one side facing the opponent rather than standing square with them.  This minimizes the opponent's chances of striking the torso to score a point.  This also allows for quick jabs with the leading hand, but it has the downside of making crosses more difficult because they will have farther to travel to reach the opponent off of their back hand.

Point sparring competitors should train for speed and accuracy, and should focus on developing quick combinations.  They should also be cognizant of how they begin each round.  It is very easy to fall into a routine of always leading with a certain technique or two.  Because a point sparring match will be stopped and restarted many times before the match is complete, a good fighter should be sure to vary attacks in order to keep the opponent guessing.

For more information on point sparring, talk to your instructor.  Seminars are also usually taught on point sparring at both Summer and Winter Camp.

# Jissen Kumite (Full Contact Fighting)

Traditional Yoshukai kumite is considered full contact. Full contact means that punches and kicks are not pulled when fighting. Fighters are allowed to make actual contact with their opponent. The rules for full contact or knockdown kumite were devised by Yoshukai founder Katsuoh Yamamoto. Master Yamamoto worked with Kyokushin karate founder Masutatsu Oyama to devise the rules for this type of competition during the 1960's. During the early years of karate competition, opponents would face each other and attack/defend without making contact. This type of kumite was known as sun dome. Fighters could attack at full speed and force, but must stop short of making contact. This type of kumite was based on the ikken hissatsu (one strike certain death) principle. At one time, practitioners believed that if they made contact during kumite that they could kill their opponent. Soke Yamamoto realized that this was not true and that training in full contact fighting was the closest way to approximate an actual fight. Today there are many styles that fight under knockdown karate rules. Some of these styles include: Yoshukai, Kyokushinkai, Oyama Karate, Enshinkaikan, Byakurenkaikan, Shidokan, and Seidokaikan.

## Rules

The legal techniques for knockdown kumite are as follows: any hand strike, closed or opened may be delivered to any area on the front of the opponent's body. This includes the chest/sternum, the solar plexus/torso area, as well as the ribs. Any kicking technique (including knees) to the head, body, or legs is legal, as well as sweeping techniques. Illegal techniques include hand techniques of any kind, including elbow strikes to the face or head. No direct kicks to the joints or groin are allowed in knockdown kumite.

The rules set for tournaments may vary depending on the organization that is putting on the event. In the early days of full contact karate tournaments, grabbing and throwing were allowed. Today's Yoshukai knockdown tournaments do not allow grabbing or throwing of any kind.

## Matches

Yoshukai knockdown matches consist of one 3 minute continuous round. If, at the end of the first round, there is no winner declared, then the fighters will fight a 2 minute overtime round. If, at the end of the 2 minute overtime, no winner is declared, then the match will extend into a final 1 minute overtime round. If the match is still a draw at the end of all 3 rounds, then the lighter fighter will be declared the winner.

Points in knockdown kumite follow the wazaari/ippon(half point/full point) system. Fighters can win a match by scoring 1 full point (ippon) or by scoring 2 half points (wazaari). A full point is awarded for any legal technique that knocks out/down your opponent for more than 3 seconds. A wazaari is awarded for any legal technique that stuns/damages or knocks down your opponent for less than 3 seconds. Sweeps followed up with a controlled punch can also be awarded a wazaari. Judges must pay close attention to determine the difference between a sweep/knock down and a trip or a slip. A fighter can also win/lose on penalties.

The penalties for committing fouls in a Yoshukai knockdown tournament are as follows. If a competitor throws an illegal technique maliciously or intentionally the striker can be immediately disqualified from the competition. When a fighter commits an incidental violation a warning is given. If 2 warnings are given in the same round, a wazaari is awarded to the other fighter. If a fighter receives a third warning in the same round, the other fighter will receive ippon and be declared the winner. At the end of each round all points and warnings/penalties are wiped clean.

## Judging

Judging in Yoshukai knockdown tournaments consist of a 5-man team. This team includes: the center judge (shushin) and 4 corner judges (shinpan). Judges for knockdown tournaments are there to ensure the fighters' safety and to enforce the rules. Each judge uses 2 flags, one red (aka) and one white (shiro), and a whistle. The color of the flags corresponds to the color sash worn by each fighter. It is important to note that the most important role of the judges in knockdown karate is to keep the fighters safe. When a judge fails to blow their whistle and halt the action after a damaging blow, it could cause undue injury to the competitor if the fight is not stopped in a reasonable amount of time. It is important to note that the judges must use the whistle along with the flags when making a call. The whistle is what tells the center judge (shinpan) to cause a halt in action.

Flag position for ippon (red wins)          Flag position for wazaari (red awarded)

Flag position for penalty (red penalized)

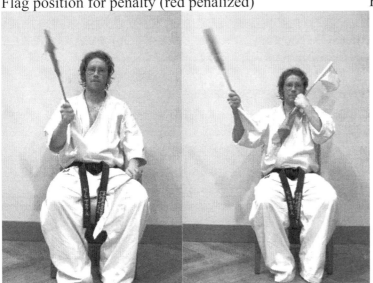

Flag position for no call (wave back and forth)

## Beginning/Ending a Match

When a knockdown karate match is getting ready to begin, two fighters' names will be called and the fighters will make their way to the center ring. The fighter on the right side of the center judge, facing the head table will be the red fighter (aka). The fighter to the left of the center judge, facing the head table will be the white fighter (shiro). At this time the center judge, as well as the 4 corner judges, are already in position. On the command from the center judge the fighters will bow to the head table. The command for this is "shomen ni rei" (bow to the front). Then the fighters will turn and on the command of "shushin ni rei" will bow to the center judge. The fighters then face each other and on the command of "otagai ni rei" they will bow to each other. Then on the command of "kamaete" the two fighters assume their respective fighting stance. Once the judge gives the command of "hajime" the match begins and the fighters engage.

Ending the match is very similar to beginning the match. Once a fighter has been declared the winner, whether by ippon/wazaari or by hantei (judges decision), the two fighters will once again face the head table. On the command "shomen ni rei" the fighters will bow to the head table. On the command of "shushin ni rei" the fighters then turn and bow to the center referee. On the final command of "otagai ni rei" the fighters then bow to each other and shake hands. It is expected that all Yoshukai fighters then go across the mat to shake the hand of the coach of the opposing fighter. The two fighters then move to an edge of the matt and bow before exiting the fighting area. Fighters will follow this same format during every match of a tournament.

## Training

Training for a Japanese full contact tournament requires additional training beyond regular class. During these additional training sessions it is good to focus on the following: cardiovascular endurance, bag/mitt training, body conditioning, and actual fighting.

Cardiovascular endurance is critical to this type of fighting. Fighters must be sure that they can last the entire fight and then some. A great way to build cardiovascular endurance for knockdown karate is wind sprints. Distance running can also be useful, but a sprint more closely resembles the short high intensity rounds of knockdown kumite. Another great way to build cardiovascular endurance is bag and mitt work.

Bag/mitt work not only builds cardiovascular endurance, but also helps in body conditioning as well as building strength in your techniques. In order to build the muscles in your hands, wrists, feet, and legs students must learn to hit with maximum impact. There are a few different ways to train with bags and mitts. Heavy bags are great for solo training in the sense that one does not have to have someone holding the bag. Heavy bags allow for complete 360 degree movement for throwing techniques. Another great tool for mitt training is a kick shield. Unlike with the heavy bag, a kick shield usually requires a partner. Using the kick shield is great for work on single techniques as well as combinations. Kick shields are great for building up the muscles in your wrist so that you can withstand the recoil from the impact of your punches. You can tell very quickly if you are not hitting correctly.

Impact/body conditioning for knockdown fighting can be done in a number of ways. Students can do timed rounds of incremental punching/kicking exercises. These exercises require at least 2 people. One person will be the striker for the entire round and the other person will be the receiver. One minute rounds work best for this exercise. When the timer starts, the striker begins throwing punches easy at first and increases the power after every punch. Once the receiver can take no more, the striker starts back over with easy strikes and gradually increases power until the receiver says stop. This process will repeat for one minute. At the end of the 1 minute round, the attacker and receiver will swap roles. This type of impact conditioning can also be used for low kicks to the legs, as well as rib level kicks. Impact/body conditioning plays a pivotal role when sparring in class and in a tournament match.

Of all the training that one must do in order to prepare for jissen kumite, nothing is more important than actual fighting. Contact sparring is where you put all of your tools together. The combinations practiced with bags/mitts, all the running, and body conditioning all plays a role in fighting. Although the other parts of the training are important, full contact sparring is essential to practice performing under pressure. Some days the sparring can be light, but other days require a hard fight to simulate an actual match. There is nothing worse than really getting hit hard for the first time in a tournament setting. The best way to train to fight, is to fight.

### Semi-Knockdown Rules – Variant 1

The legal techniques for this variation are as follows: any hand strike, closed or opened may be delivered to any area on the front of the opponent's body except the head. This includes the chest/sternum, the solar plexus/torso area, as well as the ribs. Any kicking technique (including knees) to the body or legs is legal, as well as sweeping techniques. Illegal techniques include *techniques of any kind*, including elbow strikes, kicks, etc. to the *face or head*. No direct kicks to the joints or groin are allowed.

### Semi-Knockdown Rules – Variant 2

The legal techniques for this variation are as follows: any hand strike, closed or opened may be delivered to any area on the front of the opponent's body except the head. This includes the chest/sternum, the solar plexus/torso area, as well as the ribs. Any *kicking* technique (including knees) to the *head*, body, or legs is legal, as well as sweeping techniques. Illegal techniques include *hand* techniques of any kind, including elbow strikes, to the *face or head*. No direct kicks to the joints or groin are allowed.

# Ippon Kumite

The purpose of ippon kumite ("one step sparring") is to teach timing and distancing. These patterns incorporate elements of self-defense, such as joint locks and takedowns, which help teach body mechanics. They also drill specific conditioned reactions in the student, so they may react appropriately without having to think if attacked.

To begin ippon kumite, students line up facing each other in pairs. One student is considered to be the defensive partner (tori) and the other the offensive partner (uke). The instructor calls out "ippon kumite," then orders, "kumite!" The defensive partner steps out into ready stance (uchihachiji dachi) and executes a double down block (morote gedan uke). The offensive partner then steps back into left foot forward front stance (hidari ashi zenkutsudachi) and executes a left hand down block (hidari te gedan uke).

The instructor will then tell under blackbelt students to get their distance. The offensive partner then steps forward into a right foot forward front stance (migi ashi zenkutsudachi) and executes a face punch (jodan zuki) to ensure they are close enough to threaten the defensive partner but not close enough to make contact. The offensive partner then steps back into their left foot forward front stance (hidari ashi zenkutsudachi) and executes a left hand down block (hidari te gedan uke).

When the instructor gives the count for ippon kumite, the offensive partner steps in and attacks with a kiai. The defensive partner executes their routine, finishing with a kiai on the last technique. In all cases, the defensive partner maintains the position they end up in until the instructor calls "back" or a similar command.

At the end of ippon kumite, if partners have gone up to number 3 or less, they should yame as usual. If they have done number 4 or 5, the instructor calls "return," "step up," or a similar command and both bring the back foot up into ready stance (uchihachiji dachi) and executes a double down block (morote gedan uke). When the instructor calls "yame," the attacker performs yame normally and defender mirrors attacker (moves right foot instead of left to come into attention stance (musubidachi)). Throughout ippon kumite, defender follows attacker. Defender waits for attacker to move for each technique, and also for circling after completing number 5.

Ippon kumite should be practiced throughout a student's training in Yoshukai. Students should refine their skill and precision. At blackbelt, students should not have to step through to get distance– they should be aware of their distance and adjust accordingly. As students progress in rank, they should also focus on executing good takedown maneuvers and proper falling technique. Defensive partners should not simply 'go' with a technique if it is poorly executed. Offensive partners should not have their resistance or power at the highest level, as injury to the defensive partner may occur. If a defender goes to a kneeling position, they must keep their back straight and be on the ball of the kneeling foot. The target when attacking from a kneeling position is always the head.

Falling description

In ippon kumite, the attacker (uke) is sometimes required to fall to the ground to complete the sequence. Proper falling technique is essential to minimize the likelihood of serious injury, such as fracture of a bone or dislocation of a joint. To execute a side fall (ippon kumite 3 and 4), the uke reaches across their body with the left hand and lowers their body to the floor with their right leg. As the uke's bottom hits the floor, they roll backwards onto their side. As the shoulder touches, the left arm extends and 'slaps' the floor with the palm down. This disperses energy away from delicate structures and to more durable parts of the body, and also disperses force over a wide area. The uke should NOT extend their arm behind them to 'catch' them as they fall– this places a significant amount of stress on the extended arm and can lead to injury.

## Ippon Kumite One

Attacker steps in with a face punch and kiai. Defender turns into a left shoulder stance and executes a right upper block. Defender turns into a right shoulder stance and executes a left middle punch outside the body. Defender turns into a left shoulder stance and executes a right upper punch outside the head followed by a right round kick and kiai. Return Count: Defender returns to ready stance with a double downward block and kiai.

## Ippon Kumite Two

Attacker steps in with a center punch and kiai. Defender steps to right into scissor stance and executes an deflecting block with the bottom of the right forearm. Defender reaches over blocking hand with left hand and grabs the attacker's wrist. With the right hand, defender executes a backfist to the attacker's temple. Defender places both thumbs on the back of attacker's hand, shifts left foot forward, and steps back into a front stance at a 45 degree angle to the offensive partner with the right foot while executing a wrist lock. Defender then executes a front kick to the side of attacker's head and kiai. Return Count: Both return to starting position and kiai.

## Ippon Kumite Three

Attacker steps in with a face punch and kiai. Defender steps back with their right foot into a modified boxing stance and executes a right knife hand block, chambering the hand to the left shoulder before the block. Defender passes attacker's wrist into left hand and raises attacker's arm up. Defender steps under attacker's arm and ends up behind them in a right defensive straddle stance while still gripping the attacker's wrist in their right hand. Defender pivots into a front stance while executing a left forearm strike to the attacker's elbow with kiai. Defender then grabs attacker's shoulder and throws them with minor outer reap. Defender follows attacker down with right knee down sword stance and executes a right face punch with kiai, then brings right fist to tsuki and left hand down to cover the attacker's face. Return Count: Both return to starting position and kiai.

## Ippon Kumite Four

Attacker steps in with a face punch and kiai. Defender executes an upper cross backhand block with the right hand closer to the defender's head. Defender circles with attacker's hand trapped clockwise to defender's left. Defender steps slightly in with left foot and executes round kick to attacker's head with right leg. Without setting the foot down, attacker executes major outer reap with the right leg while striking the attacker's adjacent shoulder with a palm heel. Defender goes down with attacker, controlling the attacker's right arm, and applies a wrist lock and a straight arm bar over the defender's left upper leg. Defender executes a right face punch with kiai, then brings right fist to tsuki. Return Count: Both come up into defensive straddle stance with left foot forward while executing a slow double knifehand block.

## Ippon Kumite Five

Attacker executes right shin kick to defender's thigh with kiai and places the foot forward into a fighting stance after kicking. Defender lifts left leg up in a shin block and steps back, switching so the left foot is back. Defender executes left shin kick to the attacker's right thigh and places the left foot forward after kicking. Attacker executes a backfist strike to defender's temple. Defender blocks with left hand outside center block. Defender sweeps attacker's arm down to attacker's right side and executes an elbow strike to the attacker's chest with a kiai. Defender then grabs the base of attacker's neck with their right hand fingers and, pushing back with the left hand, sweeps their right leg around into a left foot forward front stance facing 180 degrees away and throwing the attacker with forward throw. Defender then moves in to attacker, kneels down with the right leg in sword stance, and executes a right face punch with kiai, then brings right fist to tsuki and left hand down to cover the attacker's face. Return Count: Both come up into defensive straddle stance with left foot forward while executing a slow double knifehand block. Both circle to right until they have returned to original positions. Finish Count: Both students bring back leg up to uchihachijidachi and execute double down block. Yame: Attacker performs yame normally, defender performs yame moving right foot instead of left foot.

# Self-Defense

Self-defense is the term generally used when applying martial arts techniques to a more real-world scenario or simulation. It includes blocks, strikes, locks, throws, chokes, and similar techniques which can harm or disable an opponent. Self-defense is taught throughout a student's Yoshukai training. When testing for 3rd kyu green belt, a self defense routine is required for promotion.

When working on self-defense techniques, consider whether the technique is best for the student. A technique that a large student employs may not be as effective in the hands of a small student, and visa versa. Also consider how the technique may need to change if your opponent is smaller or larger than you. Become proficient in a handful of techniques that work well for your style, rather than trying to learn a wide breadth of techniques. Obviously, as the student progresses in rank, they will acquire more self-defense techniques and strategies, and so improve their breadth.

In a real-world self-defense situation, the most important thing is your safety and the safety of others. The best situations are those which are avoided entirely. Being aware of your surroundings will help you avoid potential confrontations. If you cannot avoid a confrontation, escape is your best option. Any physical conflict has a chance for injury, so escape is better than fighting. If you cannot escape, diffusing the situation is best. Only if all else fails should you resort to physical violence.

Physical violence can be subdivided into two categories: life-threatening and non-life-threatening. An example of the latter is if you are accosted in a bar by someone who is obviously impaired. In this case, it is unlikely that they are trying to seriously harm or kill you. Techniques differ depending on the situation. In a non-life-threatening situation, a lock or pain compliance technique may be appropriate. Only use locks and similar techniques if you have complete control over the situation. If you feel that your life is in danger, you must employ techniques which are universally effective and devastating. If your life is in danger, a good maxim to work from is, "When in doubt, hit."

## Self-Defense Routines

To test to 3rd kyu green belt, and for each test thereafter, a student must design a series of 5 routines with an attacker, simulating a real-world self-defense situation. The student ("tori") should work with one (or two for Shodan and higher tests) individual(s) (called the "uke") on their routine. When presenting the routine, the uke and tori approach the judges. The tori calls "kiyotsuke" and all partners come to attention. The tori calls "rei" and all partners bow. All partners then step out into a ready stance and execute a double down block. The tori introduces themselves and asks for permission to begin. All partners then yame and move to the starting position. The partners face each and the tori calls "rei" and all partners bow. The tori then calls "hajime" or "kumae" and the sequence begins. At the end, all partners yame to each other and bow, then turn and bow to the judges.

For each routine within the set, the uke should initiate an attack. This can be a grab, push, punch, kick, etc. From there, the tori should respond. A response might be to release (in the case of a grab), to block, to dodge, to meet the attacker's force, or to take the attacker's force. Thereafter, the tori executes techniques with precision and control.

Within the routine, typically near the end, tori executes a technique which brings uke to the ground. This can be a powerful hand technique or kick or an execution of a throw. Once uke is on the ground, tori will typically deliver a final technique to ensure that the uke is defeated.

Each routine should flow relatively smoothly from one to the next. Do not take excessive time setting up each routine. Safety for the uke is extremely important, and improper execution or poor control can lead to injury. The techniques need to be executed with intensity, but without harm to the uke. This may require you to pull techniques, particularly strikes to the head, joints, and groin. Tori and uke should work together to make sure each routine is practiced and comfortable for both parties. Certain uke can receive different techniques than other uke (especially falls and throws), so if the uke must change, practice with the uke involved is essential.

# Combinations

Combinations are a set of movements designed to mimic what a martial arts practitioner would use in a fighting situation. Also referred to as fighting combinations, they are a group of two or more moves that flow together logically and with a specific purpose. Fighting combinations are practiced like kata, to improve muscle memory, strength, endurance, and knowledge of fighting techniques.

Training with specific combinations allows the karate practitioner to react to a situation without having to think about it. This is called "mind of no mind" and means that a person will react without having to make a conscious decision to do so. Combinations also allow karate-ka to practice new moves and learn to put them together in a way that is effective.

Specific combinations are taught and required at each rank from 10th kyu to 1st kyu. These combinations build upon techniques and skills that you have learned at that specific rank and the ranks below it. The student should be able to do the combinations for their current rank and all the ranks below them. Below are the combinations that are required for each rank.

## 10th Kyu to 8th Kyu

1. Front kick, step forward, round kick, step forward
2. Round kick, skip sidekick
3. Step forward down block in boubi shikodachi, reverse punch into zenkutsudachi

## 8th Kyu to 7th Kyu

1. Front leg front kick, back leg round kick, step forward reverse punch
2. Round kick, step forward, skip sidekick, backfist
3. Slide forward jab, reverse punch

## 7th Kyu to 6th Kyu

1. Slide forward backfist, reverse punch, round kick
2. Step forward down block in boubi shikodachi, reverse punch into zenkutsudachi, spin forward side kick
3. Outside crescent kick, front kick, step forward

## 6th Kyu to 5th Kyu

1. Front foot round kick, skip side kick, reverse punch
2. Double round kick, step forward, skip hook kick
3. Slide forward jab, reverse punch, hook with forward hand, uppercut with back hand

## 5th Kyu to 4th Kyu

1.  Knee block, back fist, reverse punch, front kick, jump front kick
2.  Slide forward spearhand strike, grab, knee strike, front kick, step forward
3.  Slide forward jab, reverse punch, ridge hand, back spinning side kick

## 4th Kyu to 3rd Kyu

1.  Front kick, spinning back hook kick, round kick (all same foot)
2.  Front kick, flying side kick, reverse punch
3.  Slide back, down block in boubi shikodachi, backfist, reverse punch into zenkutsudachi, ridge hand, forward spinning hook kick

## 3rd Kyu to 2nd Kyu

1.  Slide forward, back fist, step forward, knifehand strike, back spinning backfist
2.  Round kick, tornado kick, backfist, reverse punch
3.  Slide back, outside center block in boubi shikodachi, backfist, reverse punch, front spinning hook kick/round kick, step forward

## 2nd Kyu to 1st Kyu

1.  Round Kick, spinning crescent kick, backfist, reverse punch
2.  Grab, step forward, elbow strike, step forward into scissor stance, rolling backfist
3.  Front kick, back kick, forward spinning side kick (all with same leg without putting foot down)

## 1st Kyu to Shodan

When testing for shodan you are required to have 5 combinations with 5 different techniques each. In each combination there needs to be either one back spinning kick or one jumping kick. For testing purposes, make your combinations simple and straightforward, this makes them easier to memorize and perform when tired later in the test. Also remember that these are fighting combinations, the moves need to be logical and at speed. They should not be slow and pausing between each move like a kata, neither should they be so fast that you have no control and the testing board cannot see what techniques you are using.

# Breaking

The breaking of boards using various techniques is part of Yoshukai training and testing. This is done to demonstrate power, control, concentration, and technique to yourself and others. The idea being that if you are able to properly break a board with a given technique, that technique is one that can be effectively used. Breaking is also done to challenge oneself to greater speed, power, and technique.

## Breaking Safety

Before breaking techniques are discussed, safety for both the breaker and the holder or holders needs to be outlined. With the amount of force that can be created in breaking demonstrations, the chance for injury to the breaker, holders, and spectators can be significant. Full care must be taken when setting up any breaking demonstration. The primary person responsible for the safety of all concerned is the person doing the breaking and as such the breaker should take it upon himself or herself to make sure everything is set up properly.

The first thing that should be considered once holders are positioned is the space around the breaking area. With some breaks, debris has the potential to travel several yards and at a great velocity, so the area around the breaking zone should be clear of spectators out to 10 yards (30 feet) from where the breaking is taking place. Those who stay in this area need to be informed of the direction that the breaker intends to strike so they can be aware of the chance of being struck.

Second, make sure that the holder or holders are properly braced. With one holder, maker sure that the holder is prepared to receive the blow in a manner where the impact will not put the holder in danger. The holder should be set in a good stable stance where he or she will be able to provide sufficient resistance to the strike while at the same time not be harmed by it. With two holders, the inside legs are placed back so the holders are in a front stance with their back legs crossed to provide stability. The outside arms hold the bottom of the object with the inside arms holding the top so that any pieces of the object knocked upward will be deflected by the inside arms.

For the breakers part, the first thing to check is to make sure the object that is being broken is not going to injure you when you strike it. Make sure the surface is clear of debris or material that could injure you when it is struck. Also to avoid injury make sure you strike the object in the correct manner. With a punch, strike with the first two knuckles while keeping the wrist straight, this keeps the wrist locked so that is does not roll when the fist strikes the object. If the knuckles above the pinkie finger are what strike the object first, it can easily result in a broken hand. When breaking with the foot, make sure you are striking with the correct part of the foot for that technique. If kicking with a roundhouse make sure the toes are pointed so you connect with the top of the foot otherwise it can result in broken toes. When kicking with a front kick, pull the toes back and connect with the ball of the foot.

# The Force behind Breaking

Any object breaks when force applied to it exceed the stress limits of the material that it is made of. When breaking wood, the wood bends until it cracks on the opposite side of the strike, breaking from back to front. This applies to any material used, wood boards, concrete blocks, ice blocks, and even baseball bats.

Force can be simply quantified as mass x acceleration. With two objects moving at the same speed the more massive object will create more force. The reverse applies also, with two objects of the same mass the one accelerating the fastest will create more force. This theory is how a smaller person is able to generate the same amount or more force than a larger person. And this speed is on of the main goals when training for breaking.

Another thing that affects the force used in breaking is concentrating as much energy into as small an area as possible. As stated earlier, when breaking with a punch you want to strike with the first two knuckles instead of the whole hand. Besides keeping your hands from breaking, this minimizes the area that you are striking with. If you strike an object with a set speed and mass but decrease the surface are of the strike by half, you produce a four-fold increase in force.

The physics to break one board or brick are the same. But what about breaking multiple boards or bricks? The way the multiple objects break is still the same as when one object breaks. When two or more boards are placed back to back and broken, they bend just like one board does, with the board farthest away breaking first then the next closest and so on. It is important to remember is that when breaking multiple objects placed back to back, the increase in difficulty does not go up by one but increases exponentially. Breaking two boards is about three times as hard as one when placed back to back. Three boards is about six times more difficult, and so on.

To help with breaking multiple objects spaces are often used. Spacers are small objects placed between the boards on the edges to allow for easier breaking. Spacers can be anything from small blocks of wood to pencils to coins. The way the spacers work is by allowing the boards above to assist in the breaking of the boards below. When the top object breaks, it falls inward and strikes the one below it; this transfers energy to the one below, assisting in the break. Breaking multiple objects with spacers is still more difficult than breaking just one but not as difficult as not using spacers at all.

# How to Train for Breaking

There are several things a person can do that will aid in their breaking demonstrations. Kicking or punching shields or hand targets can be done to increase your control and accuracy of a technique. A makiwara, a traditional Japanese training instrument made of a wood board wrapped in rope or covered in foam that is anchored into the ground or attached to the wall, can also be used for target practice. But one of the main purposes to a makiwara is to toughen up the body. This is useful in training for breaking so that the chances for personal injury are decreased. Re-breakable boards can be used for practice and training. These are plastic boards that have a split in the middle that allow the practitioner to reuse the board over and over again. These boards also come in different thicknesses so a person can increase the challenge of their breaks.

When training for breaking for a test or demonstration be sure to practice the break well before hand as any hesitation during the actual demonstration itself can lead to mistakes that keep you from accomplishing your break. Also have your materials prepared and selected ahead of time if possible. It can help to mark each piece of material with the specific technique you will be using to break it. Doing this will allow you to make sure you break difficult materials with techniques that you are more comfortable with to increase you success.

Finally, practice, practice, practice. Breaking is not a difficult process and can be done by pretty much any martial artist, but you must be comfortable with each technique. Performing a technique you have practiced repeatedly to where you have good muscle memory will dramatically increase you chances of a successful break.

Also don't cheat, don't pre-score boards, oven dry bricks, or pre-crack wood. This may allow you to break more but it goes against the integrity and philosophy of Yoshukai. It may give the people watching the demonstration a wow factor but you will be cheating yourself.

# Breaking Requirements

Under the WYKKO, there are breaking requirements for every test. In most cases the requirements state what category of technique needs to be used, but it is left up to the person breaking which specific technique will be used. If the test requires one hand technique it can be anything from a straight punch to a palm-heel strike and the same applies to foot techniques. The only time this is not so is specifically stated. Also, each technique used needs to break only one board unless specifically stated. The breaking requirements for each rank are listed below.

### 10th kyu to 8th kyu
1 hand and 1 foot technique

### 8th kyu to 7th kyu
2 different foot techniques

### 7th kyu to 6th kyu
1 foot, 1 hand, and 1 flying side kick or jump front kick

### 6th kyu to 5th kyu
2 board side kick, 1 hand technique, and 1 jump front kick

### 5th kyu to 4th kyu
2 board side kick, 1 hand technique, and 1 back spinning kick

### 4th kyu to 3rd kyu
2 board back spinning side kick, 2 board side kick, and 1 hand technique

### 3rd kyu to 2nd kyu
2 board side kick, 1 back spinning hook kick, 1 hand technique, and 1 flying side or jump front kick

### 2nd kyu to 1st kyu
2 board side kick, 1 back spinning kick, 1 flying side or jump front kick, and 1 hand technique

### 1st kyu to Shodan
2 different hand techniques, 2 board stationary kick, 1 spinning back hook kick, and 1 jump front kick

# Terminology

## Yoshukai Terminology

Five Precepts (Shugyo sho gokun)
- Respect and manners – Reigi o omonzubeshi
- Be prudent in action – Taido o imashimubeshi
- Be prudent in speech – Gengo o tsutsushimubeshi
- Keep high spirited – Iki o sakan ni subeshi
- Keep yourself clean – Seiketsu o mune to subeshi

Yoshukai – Strive for excellence

Japanese Headquarters – Kitakyushu City, Japan

WYKKO U.S. Headquarters – Dothan, Alabama, USA

World Director – Grandmaster Katsuoh Yamamoto (10th degree blackbelt)

WYKKO U.S. Directors – Master Hiroaki Toyama (8th degree blackbelt) & Master Mike Culbreth (7th degree blackbelt)

Year Yoshukai was founded – 1963

Year Yoshukai was brought to the US – 1967

Year WYKKO was founded – 2000

Yoshukai Byword – Patience – Nin

The Way – Michi

Yoshukai Motto – Make efforts and you will achieve – Rikki hitatsu

Empty Hand – Karate

Yoshukai Emblem (Patch) – The Yata-no-kagami was one of the Three Sacred Treasures of the Imperial House. The emblem is a combination of the Japanese flag, the word Yoshukai in Japanese, and Yata-no-kagami, which symbolizes "Truth, Goodness, and Beauty" which are also reflected in this mirror.

## Commands

Bow – Rei
Prepare – Yoi
Fist-to-hip – Tsuki
Finish – Yame
Attention – Kiyotsuke
Begin – Hajime
Relax – Yasume
Turn – Mawatte
Kneel down – Seiza
Stand up – Kiritsu
Change feet – Kaete
Wait – Matte
Close eyes – Mokuso
Open eyes – Kaimoku
Call for judge's decision – Hantei
Yell ("Energy shout") – Kiai

## Striking Areas

Ball of Foot – Koshi
Instep – Haisoku
Edge of Heel – Sokuto
Heel – Kakato
Leg – Ashi
Hand – Te

## General Terminology

Instructor ("One who has gone before") – Sensei
School ("Place of the way") – Dojo
Uniform – Dogi
Belt – Obi
Black Belt – Kuroobi
Checked (black or red) Belt – Madara Obi
Standing bow – Tachirei
Kneeling bow – Zarei
Energy – Ki
Hidari – Left
Migi – Right
Blackbelt Rank – Yudansha
Good morning – Ohayo
Good afternoon – Konnichiwa
Good evening – Konban wa
Thank you – Arigato
Goodbye – Sayonara
Yes – Hai
No – Iie
Do you understand – Wakarimasu ka
I understand – Wakarimasu
How are you? – O genki desu ka
I am fine – Genki desu
Punching board – Makiwara
Breaking – Tameshiwari
The art of catching a sword with your hands – Shinkenshirahadori
Founder – Soke
Front of dojo – Shomen
Offensive partner – Tori
Defensive partner – Uke
Off-balancing – Kuzushi
Karate student – Seito
Full point – Ippon
Half point – Wazaari
Minor advantage – Youkoh or Koka
Technique – Waza
Analysis – Breakdown of the meaning of kata techniques – Bunkai
Form – Kata
Sparring – Kumite
Weapons – Kobudo
Sheath sword – Noto
Draw sword – Bato
Blood Flick – Chiburi
Focus – Kime

## Blackbelt Titles

Formal titles are used during a formal bow-in and in respectful correspondence, such as letters.  They may also be used as a form of address, particularly for Shihan.

1st and 2nd degree – Shodan and Nidan – Yudansha
3rd degree – Sandan – Sempai
4th degree – Yondan – Shihan-dai
5th degree and higher – Godan, Rokudan, Sichidan, Hachidan – Shihan
President – Kaicho
Founder – Grandmaster Yamamoto – Soke

## Forms (Kata)

Twenty-Seven Movements – Ni Ju Shichi no Kata
First Basic Form – Kihon Kata Shodan
Second Basic Form – Kihon Kata Nidan
Third Basic Form – Kihon Kata Sandan
Fourth Basic Form – Kihon Kata Yondan
Advancing and Retreating – Zen Shin Kotai
Four Directions – Shihohai
Basic Nunchaku Form – Kihon Kata Nunchaku
Thirteen Hands – Seisan
First Basic Nunchaku Form – Kihon Kata Shodan Nunchaku
First Basic Bo Form – Kihon Kata Shodan Bo
Twenty-Four Steps – Niseishi
Second Basic Bo Form – Kihon Kata Nidan Bo
Advancing and Retreating Sai – Zenshin Kotai Sai
Vision of the Crane Minor – Rohai Sho
Third Basic Bo Form – Kihon Kata Sandan Bo
Fighting to the Four Directions Sai – Shiho Hai Sai
Vision of the Crane Major – Rohai Dai
Endless/Infinity – Mugen
Twisting Body Motion – Tenshin
To Breach a Fortress – Bassai
Fighting to the East – Chinto
Ending the Morning Mist - Shounnokon
Monks of Peace – Sochin
Rolling Palsm - Tensho
Thirty-Four Hands – San Shi Ryu
Tiger Eyes – Ru San
Dragon Mountain – Ryu San
Dragon in the Sky – Un Ryu
Inspired by Kung Shang K'ung – Kusanku

## Stances (Tachi)

Front Stance – Zenkutsudachi
Offensive Straddle Stance – Kougeki shikodachi
Defensive Straddle Stance – Boubi shikodachi
Immovable Stance – Fudodachi
Ready Stance – Uchihachiji dachi
Attention Stance – Musubidachi
Forward Stance – Mae dachi
Scissor Stance – Hasamidachi
One Legged Stance – Ippon ashidachi
Parallel Stance – Heikodachi
Cat Stance – Neko ashidachi
Sword (Kneeling) Stance – Iai dachi
Horse Stance – Kibadachi
Hourglass Stance – Sanchin dachi
Back Stance – Kokutsudachi


## Blocks (Uke)

Upper Block – Jodan uke
Inside Center Block – Chuudan Uchi uke
Outside Center Block – Chuudan Soto uke
Down Block – Gedan uke
Knifehand Block – Shuto uke
Palm Heel Block – Shotei uke
Ridgehand Block – Haito uke
Elbow Block – Embi uke
Knee Block – Hiza uke
(Upper/Lower) Crosshand Block – (Jodan/Gedan) Juji uke
Knife/Open Crosshand Block – Shuto Juji uke
Back Hand Block – Haisho uke
Wedge Block – Kakiwake uke

## Strikes (Atemi)

Fist – Seiken
Upper Punch – Jodan zuki
Center Punch – Chuudan zuki
Down Punch – Gedan zuki
(Upper/Center/Down) Reverse Punch – (Jodan/Chuudan/Gedan) Gyaku zuki
(Upper/Center/Down) Same Side Punch – (Jodan/Chuudan/Gedan) Jun zuki
Knife Hand – Shuto
Inward Knife Hand – Ura shuto
Backfirst – Uraken
Palm Strike – Shotei
Ridge Hand – Haito
Elbow Strike – Embi
Knee – Hiza
Hammer Fist – Tsutsuken
Back Hand – Haisho
Bent Wrist – Koken
Spear Hand – Nukite
2 Finger Spear Hand – Nihon nukite
Head Strike – Zutsuki
Flying Knee – Tobi hiza geri
Chasing Punch – Oizuki
Bear Hand – Kumade

## Kicks (Keri)

Front Kick – Mae geri
Round Kick – Mawashi geri
Side Kick – Yoko geri
Jump Front Kick – Nidan geri
(Inside/Outside) Crescent kick – (Uchi/Soto) Ko geri
Flying Side Kick – Tobi yoko geri
Forward Spinning Side Kick – Zenpou yoko geri
Hook Kick – Kake geri
Shin Kick – Sune geri
Axe Kick – Kakato otoshi
Back Spinning Side Kick – Ushiro yoko geri
Spinning Crescent Kick – Ushiro ko geri
Tornado Kick – Tobi mawashi ko geri
(Front/Back) Spinning Hook Kick – (Zenpou/Ushiro) Kake geri
Back Kick – Ushiro geri
Jump Round Kick – Nidan mawashi geri
Jump Spinning Hook Kick – Tobi ushiro kake geri
Jump Spinning Crescent Kick – Tobi ushiro ko geri
Chasing Kick – Oigeri

## Counting

One – Ichi
Two – Ni
Three – San
Four – Shi
Five – Go
Six – Roku
Seven – Shichi
Eight – Hachi
Nine – Kyu
Ten – Ju
Twenty – Ni-Ju
Thirty – San-Ju
Fourty – Yon-Ju
Fifty – Go-Ju
Sixty – Roku-Ju
Seventy – Shichi-Ju
Eighty – Hachi-Ju
Ninety – Kyu-Ju
One Hundred - Hiyaku